Schizophrenia – The Last Taboo

David Stewart

Michael Terence Publishing

First published in paperback by
Michael Terence Publishing in 2019
www.mtp.agency

ISBN 9781913289362

Dedicated to the Southport NHS Community Mental Health Team for all of their care and support over the years.

And to also Teresa for giving me a break when no one else would…

Chapter 1

Friday, 13 December 1996

The flat was small and austere by any standards. 13 Castle Close, Southport. It was at the bottom of an alley with a leafy avenue facing the front of the property. The avenue reminded me of the kind of alley a serial killer would frequent looking for a new victim, and it added to the dismal tone of the flat. There was a living room/bedroom, a galley kitchen and a bathroom. The flat was sparsely furnished with furniture which would have been in fashion in the 1960s. There was a bed, dressing table, a padded bench to sit on, a cupboard and a dining table by the bay window with an A2 drawing board on it. There was no TV, and there was nothing homely about it, no creature comforts, and it was cold. The only heat in the living room was a calor gas heater that had a weird connector, so I could not get any gas for it, and a 1950s bar fire that used to give me the creeps, so I never turned it on. The kitchen had an electric cooker that did not work and a second-hand microwave. Hot and cold taps leaked, making an annoying hissing sound. There was a small window that I had screwed shut to stop people from getting into the flat. The bathroom had a cream suite, sink, bath and toilet and was long overdue for a makeover. This sure as hell was not home! And there was something else: it had a bad karma. I thought it was just me. Unfortunately, I found out I was right; there was something evil about the place.

I had very few friends by this time, as I was scared they would get mixed up in me. My only respite from the time-travel war was a few pints once a fortnight down my local pub, the Coronet.

Being a time agent is not as glamourous as you might think. I had no money, and I was also followed around by an evil presence. Whenever I did have money, 'it' would make me throw it away or spend it stupidly. I was terrified most of the time, but I wasn't scared of dying; it was what they would do to me if they got their hands on me before I died. Along with this, I was regularly visited by famous people, mostly women and major-league politicians, and they would also be after something. They had no sympathy for my condition by my orders. I told them if they tried to help me, it would make my situation worse. I had to get out of there without help and in the clothes I was standing up in. There was no other way.

It was a Friday night, so I was thinking of going out having just had my dole cheque. I was wearing the usual, jeans, tatty trainers and a T-shirt. All my clothes were falling to bits, and I looked like a scarecrow with my long wavy chestnut locks and catalogue jacket. The Coronet was my only escape from my personal hell. They liked me there, and it was the only place I felt free.

I was looking out the window of my flat feeling glum, and then felt the presence of someone standing behind me. I turned and recognised two men. They must have beamed in, as the door was still locked.

This was President Clinton. Clinton had been in and out of my life a few times in the past. Clinton was aware of the time-travel espionage I was caught up in. Originally I found it exciting to be involved in such a venture, but it soon lost its lustre. It was very scary at times and was like living in a dystopia no one else was aware of. It was impossible to share with others what was actually going on because it could put them in danger, and also, who the hell would believe me anyway?

The other man, well built, balding with grey hair and tall, stood beside him. This was General Schwarzkopf. I had worked with Schwarzkopf on the Mars 2 programme and corresponded with him. We both loved rockets and stealth. He first introduced himself to me in 1988 when I finished my training with the ATA as an airframe and propulsion systems fitter. I was a bit of the bad boy of my class, but I was years ahead of my classmates in some respects and figured out quite a few top-secret devices by myself without prompting, which made me useful to him. I loved being involved with new technology, and it felt great to be literally decades ahead of the man on the street. It gave me a sense of pride and made me feel very special.

I knew that it was probably bad news as soon as I recognised them. They only ever wanted me if they needed something usually of great importance. But I trusted them and that is the way it was. They had helped me in the past and were very powerful men and good allies.

Clinton spoke to me. 'David, we have some bad news. We are going to have to send you back to protect the time line. This is the only way we can win the war. If you are not sent back, infiltrators from the Star Trek faction will hold the time line and the war in the 24th century will be lost.'

'Why me?' I asked. 'Surely I can't be this important!'

'You solved the hyperdrive equation. That is why we need you to go back so it does not fall in to enemy hands first.'

I knew this day was going to come, but it was still horrifying. In fact, in the cold light of day, it was even worse. I was to be trapped forever in a time loop to protect people who would not be born for centuries. 'This is hell!' I said, 'There must be another way.'

'Sorry, son,' said Schwarzkopf. 'You are it. The Star Wars computer is going to lock onto you now.'

I could feel the transporter beam beginning to lock. It was a strange sensation not dissimilar to going down on a fast roller coaster. I could feel my earthly body ablating, and I became an entity of living energy. I could feel myself racing through time, seeing ghosts of images and people from my past. I could remember saying, 'Please, God, not again!' But I don't know if he heard my prayer. I had gone from this existence.

Friday, 13 January 1967

I was born in the unremarkable town of Blackpool, Lancashire, on a rainy January day. The only thing of any remark was the fact that it was Friday the 13th.

At 10:00 a.m. I arrived, screaming into the world and with good reason! My conscience from the future was in the back of my brain. 'Please, God, not again!' I know nobody is supposed to remember their birth, but I did. After the birth, which went smoothly, my father, in a rush, went to register my birth. He promptly forgot my middle name of Elliot, so I was just christened David Stewart.

My father was the assistant manager of the Savoy Hotel, and my mother was a receptionist from the Imperial Hotel across the road. They met each other through work. My father's side of the family had Jewish descent but had changed the family name in 1950 from Steinart to Stewart. They were originally from Austria but moved to England when the Nazis started to rise in the mid-1930s. The family split in two at that point: the Harts and the Stewarts. The Harts had all the money. My father's mother was from New Zealand. Her family, the Hoyles, originated in Bolton, Lancashire; her grandfather had been very rich. He was a mill owner and had six sons who all died of tuberculosis. He felt he was being punished by God and gave away his entire fortune to the church to try to appease God! It left the family in destitution!

My mother's side were very working class, originating in Manchester. During the war, Grandad was in the fire service in the south. He worked for ICI after the war until he retired. Grandma was in the postal service during the war and became a shop assistant and primarily a housewife and homemaker after the war.

I have one other memory of Blackpool and that is all. I remember being in my pram on Blackpool promenade trying to communicate with my future mind. I felt gagged, bound and suffocated. I could not communicate as a baby. I held my breath until I could take no more and then had to resign myself to the fact that I would not be able to communicate. My old living energy then hid in the back of my mind and would not be awoken again for another 12 years.

In November 1968, we moved to Filey in Yorkshire, where my father was offered his first job as general manager of a hotel. I remember bits from this time as my conscience began to develop. I remember having a haircut and it being paid for in old money. I also remember my father's car, a green MGB GT with soft top and wire wheels. When I mentioned this to him years later, he was surprised I could remember this! We lived in an apartment in the hotel, it was dark and uninviting. It made the black-and-white TV scarier. I used to hide behind the sofa when *Doctor Who* was on in black-and-white with Patrick Trouton. My parents used to find this funny.

My mother was very proactive with me trying different music. She played me a variety of music to see which type I liked. The most memorable ones were Prokofiev's 'Peter and the Wolf' and the Beatles, Eleanor Rigby. Also Tom Jones, 'What's New Pussycat' and Petula Clark's 'Down Town'. 'Down Town' was my favourite at the time, but Eleanor

Rigby stayed with me the longest. As I got better at song writing, this became my favourite and something to aspire to.

One afternoon, I was playing with my Action Men in my room. My father was working, and my mother was attending to my sister in the other bedroom. Happily in a world of my own, I saw the bedroom door close behind me. I assumed it was my mother or the wind. I looked over my shoulder and discovered I had a 'visitor' in my room. It was a large gelatinous blob basically about six feet across straddling my bed. It had an enormous head and a large slobbering mouth. Its skin was brown and glistened in the dim light of my room. There was also a smell which I had never smelled before. A cross between straw, animals and my mother's makeup. He told me he was my nemesis. He told me I had done him wrong in another lifetime and that I was going to pay for what I had done to him. Obviously I had no idea what he was talking about. I told him, 'I don't know who you are'. He told me, 'I am Jabba the Hutt and I will come to get you in the future. You cannot escape. You will pay!' I was very disturbed by the whole thing but found it impossible to talk to my parents about because it was so bizarre. I think I got a 'There, there, never mind, David, it was just a nightmare'. My fingers were crossed that my parents were right.

Autumn 1970 we moved to Poole in Dorset. My father was now manager of the Roundhouse Hotel in the centre of town. We lived in a nice apartment on the top floor of the hotel, and by 1972, we had a colour TV. The furniture was very modern; I think most of it were probably supplied by the hotel owners. I had my first proper bedroom with Disney bed linen. The view from the living room was a building site. The most notable feature was the tall yellow cranes from Lange Construction.

While at the Roundhouse, I used to get nightmares about a little plane that used to terrify me for some reason. It came from the credits of a TV programme called *Play Away*. I think this could have had something to do with the 11 years I spent in the aviation industry coming back to haunt me. The dreams persisted until I left Poole. I also used to get bad dreams about getting sucked down transparent pipes full of water, and there was no way out for me. But there was this man called David Henry Cooper (something to do with the boxer?) who found a way out. I was always trying to get his help.

As a boy, I loved watching TV especially as we had a colour set. I particularly enjoyed football and motor racing (I wanted to be a racing driver). I also found the news fascinating. Stories of the Cold War, Vietnam, Northern Ireland and the Apollo programme – I found these captivating. I would get sent to bed at seven every night apart from Star Trek night when I was allowed to stay up until 8:00 p.m. I loved Star Trek and used to fantasise about travelling the galaxy in my own spaceship.

My fifth birthday was very memorable for all of the wrong reasons! My dad invited everyone from my class to the hotel for a party. The kids ran riot, running around screaming and bothering the guests. Staff were worn out having to chase the kids down and get them back into the party room. We had a

Punch and Judy man who had a Dalek, which I thought was brilliant. Lots of jelly and ice cream. One of the staff swung me round by my legs, which was like being at the fair, and everyone else wanted to have a go. I had a great day. For some reason, my father blamed me for all the chaos that ensued and never forgave me. I was only five for God's sake!

Also on my fifth birthday, my mother told me that I could have anything I wanted if I sold my soul. She explained it was the inner magic of your being and was very valuable. She also warned me to never ask for more (especially seven wishes). My mum told me everyone does this and said you will get your soul back; most people do. So there was the big decision: what did I want? I thought about it and then decided. 'I want to sell my soul to win the war.' My mother was taken aback. She said it was very noble of me and she was proud of me.

Summer 1972, I was watching football on television. I was on my own. My sister was out with the nanny; my mum and dad were working in the hotel. The picture became fuzzy, and at first I thought there was something wrong with the set. The picture began to reform to a man in a blue uniform with gold braids on his shoulders and cap. 'This is a priority transmission. This is Lockheed Skunk Works. Our star ships are ready. We have perfected star drive, and we are leaving for Proxima Centauri. Our mission is to set up a base on Mars 2. This will be earth's guard dog. Using ripple radar, we have detected star drive operating not of this Earth in our sector, and we are going to investigate. Our mission may be the most important mission man has ever made. May God guide and protect us.' I saw men in the blue uniforms being beamed up like in *Star Trek*, but this looked real. The screen went fuzzy again, and normal service then resumed. I asked a few people over the years if they remembered this transmission, but I never met anyone else who remembered watching this. I realised from seeing that I had a new dream of becoming an astronaut and exploring other worlds. Now it was a real possibility and not just a childish distraction. To be honest, I was not excited by the Apollo missions; they were small compared to this. My head was in the clouds now, and I began to see science fiction in a new light. Rather than fiction, I saw it as possible although I fervently believed time travel was impossible. I was profoundly impressed by this tour de force of Lockheed Skunk Works technology.

I enjoyed school very much. I went to St Monica's junior school, which was a Catholic school, from September 1972. In my class, there were about 20 of us: 10 boys and 10 girls. I had one main friend, David Scott (like the astronaut – I was a bit jealous because he had a cool name). My main activities were painting pictures, *Janet and John* books and fighting anyone who wanted a fight under the teacher's piano. In short, I was a bit of a bad boy. I used to bite people too. Occasionally we went to church as a class. At the time, I was undecided whether or not I believed in God. As I was not a Catholic, I got segregated from the other children. While they were getting the 'holy bread' and a blessing, I had to stand at the back. This felt so unfair, and why were these people special and I was not? I think if I had been given the holy bread, I would have believed from there on in. That did it for me, and I rejected God and Christianity for leaving me out. I felt like this about God for many years. I felt betrayed and unworthy.

Christmas 1972 was one of the best. I was free and very happy with life. On Christmas morning, I was up at the obligatory 4:00 a.m. and ran straight to the tree to get my presents. There was nothing there! I was heartbroken. What had I done wrong?! My sisters' presents were there. I started to cry when my father came into the room. I asked him, 'Daddy, why don't I have any presents?' 'Go back to your room, David. They are under the bed.' I went for a look and there they were. I was ecstatic! I got everything I asked for and more! Matchbox cars and track, Lego, and some really good books with pictures in. I was a very happy boy.

This was the last Christmas I spent in Poole. Things were about to change. Some for the better and some for the worst, but this would define me and make me who I am today.

13 January 1973

This was my sixth birthday, and my parents had news for me. We were moving to Glasgow in Scotland, and I would be going to an all-boys prep school in Moffatt, Dumfries, called St Ninians. I felt excitement and also trepidation. This was the first major change in my life.

My father had been offed a new-build hotel in Glasgow with Rio Stakis to get the business up and running. The hotel was called the Vincent, and it was in the centre of the city. My father and mother were over the moon. A new start and a significant pay rise for my father. We also bought a house in Bears Den, which was a bit of a posh area. Things were going well.

We moved to Scotland in February 1973. The preparation for school began in earnest. We had to go to special approved outfitters to get the uniform and the trunk. These shops were not cheap. I needed full uniform, sportswear, shoes of various types. Also a kilt. There was no Royal Stewart kilt in my size, so my father bought me a girls 'skirt' instead despite my objections. He used his classic line: 'What bloody difference does it make!' This would come back to bite him on the arse a couple of times in the future.

I was a bit worried about the new school. Changing school is very stressful especially for a six-year-old. Being told it was a boarding school made it worse. My mother assured me that it would be fine, and I would make new friends and have a good time. I wasn't so sure.

The day finally came. It was time to bite the bullet and start.

Sunday, 29 April 1973

First impressions of the area were good. The village that the school was in was very picturesque and small. There were a few shops mostly for passing tourists. The school was hidden from the main road and was accessed by a narrow road. The first thing that struck me was the wall that surrounded the school. It was tall, stone and topped with broken glass held on by cement. The drive was gravel, and you could hear the crunching under the wheels of my father's Capri. There were trees over the drive, and I noted with excitement that they were conker trees. The building was in two parts. A large red brick building was on the left, which had dormitories and was linked by a wooden bridge to the main building. The main entrance was quite ostentatious but inviting. As we pulled in, some of the boys were milling around and they looked older than me. My mum told me not to worry. There are lots of boys my age, and I will be able to play football with them. A couple of prefects met us at the door. They were expecting me. I said my goodbyes to my parents and sister. My mother was quite tearful. I saw them driving away and my heart sank. I would not see my mum and dad for 10 weeks. The prefects took my trunk to my dorm, and I tagged along in silence. One of the prefects was called Ian Crossen; his nickname was Grassy. I looked up to him, and he was the first friend I made at this new school. We went up some stairs and across the bridge was the dorm block. My dorm was on the end. There were eight beds of boys, all my age. The room was big and airy; it had a good vibe. So I thought. He said to me, 'Welcome to Colditz'.

The prefects left me in the room to get acquainted with my buddy, Bishop. As I discovered to my horror, all the boys addressed each other by surname. Bishop was about the same age as me. He started at St Ninians in September 1972 at age five! At the time it seemed normal, but looking back, five is a very young age to leave home and go to boarding school.

I had a million questions. 'When do we play football?' 'We don't', said Bishop. 'We play rugger here. We do sport every Wednesday and Saturday afternoons. We also attend classes on Saturday mornings.' I was horrified. My mother assured me we would play football, which I loved. Also working on a Saturday!

Bishop helped me learn the rules. There was a rule for everything. First, he helped me set up my bed area, everything in its place; it was like the army. The trunk was at the end of the bed. Toothbrush and paste on the bedside table. The bed was made to perfection, something Bishop helped me with. I was then shown the bathroom. It was cold and white and very uninviting especially at 7:00 a.m. when we were getting up.

The dorm area was under the watchful eye of the matron, a horrible old hag who had a reputation of hitting boys over the head with a cricket shoe. Although it was always a friend of a friend who this had happened to. I was not going to mess with her! Bishop then showed me round the school.

It had an unusual layout with two main buildings. Accommodation and labs to the left and classrooms, library and dinner hall to the right. First, we went down to the lab on the ground level. There were two lab stroke science rooms. One was a classroom with Bunsen burners and fitted tables with stools around them and a big blackboard at one end. There was also a periodic table on the walls and various other colourful posters of stars and planets. This was my favourite room. The other room opposite had massive frogs in tanks. I wondered why they were there. It must have been a hobby of one of the teachers. In the hall that connected the two rooms there was a piano. There was only one rule with pianos at the school: no playing 'Chopsticks'!

We then went up a flight of stairs to the bridge, which bought us into the main school building. We started on the ground floor. Again, there was a small hall with the 'War Room'. This was Master Monty's classroom where war, Latin and classics were taught. Bishop then showed me something on the wall. This was the conduct mark chart for all 68 students. You could get good conduct marks and bad conduct marks. Good conduct marks were like hen's teeth. Bad conduct marks were easy to obtain! Bishop explained that if you got six good conduct marks, you got a prize. If you got six bad conduct marks, you were sent to the office of the headmaster, Spongey Spencer. He was camp commandant and very strict. Bishop told me that he gave different punishments depending on how merciful he was feeling. The worst was a tossup between the horse crop and the wooden shoe, then came the training shoe and lastly the slipper.

We walked down a corridor to the main entrance hall in silence and single file. You could get reprimanded for talking, running or going the wrong way. We walked past two classrooms. The one on the right would be my main classroom, Fourth Form. Then a few meters past, this was Spongey Spencer's office. Opposite his door was the entrance to the changing rooms and showers. This was even stricter than the corridors and felt like martial law. Anything left on the floor would get you a first-class ticket to Spongey's office.

We then crossed the main entrance hall past the main staircase, which was very imposing and made of dark hardwood with a carpet held by brass fittings. The study was to the right, and the kitchens and main dining hall were down a narrow corridor. The main hall had five long tables. At the back, there was a table in line with the corridor and then three side-by-side at 90 degrees then another in line with the first. This was the head table where the teachers sat and Spongey's daughter Lady Jane, who was the only girl at the school being educated there even though this was a boy's school. Around the hall were wooden placards with the names of ex-students who died during the two world wars, all officers and very young.

We then went back to the main entrance hall and upstairs to the library. This was the nicest room in the school where we could actually relax. I noted there were a lot of strange pictures round the school of old people from decades ago. They all seemed to be staring at you and the eyes followed you as you walked past. It was creepy. The library was one of the only places in the school with a working TV. I was almost pleased until Bishop told me that we were only allowed to watch Rugby Special on a Sunday evening and that was all. I was horrified. No football too; that was apparently a trog's game. On the upside, the library was the most comfortable room in the school and our only haven as students. Trogs was the name that the boys called the local children who did not go to the school because they were in the Dark Ages compared to us although the masters did not like us doing this and would tell us not to.

Bishop took me to the back of the school and showed me the woodworking shop. There students made stilts and bird tables. I think they used to bill parents for the wood. This was another cold and uninviting room, which seemed to be the tone of the whole place, cold and uninviting.

Lastly, Bishop took me up to the crow's nest. The captain lived up there. I never actually figured out what it was that the captain really did; I think he may have retired. But the best bit was his train set. It was massive and awesome. I noted it was an old-style set with a three-rail track, the layout being about 15 feet long and filling most of the room. Every little boy's dream. There were shunting sheds, platforms, lots of locomotives and rolling stock and long express ways and tunnels. This was a nice place to visit last.

It was 5:00 p.m. and the dinner gong went. Bishop took me down to the main hall and showed me my place. My napkin ring was at my setting. This is where I met the other boys.

I sat in the middle of two other boys on a bench: Bishop and Roper, an American lad. They were both in my class, and we became good friends. We were all a little naughty at times, which was what we had in common. They had been at the school for six months more than me.

We were tightly packed on the benches, and it was impossible to raise your elbows to eat, my first lesson in etiquette. Although the meals were awful, they were treated with the reverence of a five-star dinner. It was the start of a new term, and the prefects at the head of the tables would propose toasts to hard work and comradery with glasses of water. It all seemed a bit silly to me. The teachers were at the head table and Lady Jane sat with them; she was 12 at that time. I am not sure if I was paranoid, but I swear that she used to stare at me. It made me feel both uncomfortable and special at the same time. We would both get acquainted.

Our first meal was Haggis. I never had it before. 'When in Scotland', said one of the other boys. It was actually quite nice. The bread was like door stops. The crust was very thick and salty. They made it on the premises. But I enjoyed it with a thick layer of butter. The meal was served with military precision. And you could set your watch by it. Some restaurants could learn a thing or two about how to serve 80 people.

After dinner, we had some time to ourselves, and Bishop and Roper took me to the library to meet some of the other boys. There was a good comradery at the school. We were all in the same boat, and the enemy was the Master. This was Colditz. This reputation was a very accurate reflection on the regime. The school was notorious for all the wrong reasons and well earned its nickname. It may have appeared funny to an outsider, but to us it was a harsh Dickensian reality.

Chapter 2

The buzzer went at 7:00 a.m. sharp. Everyone got up straightaway and headed to the bathroom in their pyjamas. It was cold; it was always cold even in the summer. We walked across the hall to our bathroom. There were three sinks, and we took turns to wash and brush our teeth under the beady eye of the matron. This was mostly conducted in silence. After washing, we got dressed and made our beds. Everything had its place. Flannel, toothbrush, soap and toothbrush and paste on the bedside cabinet. Shoes at the foot of the bed and clothes in the cabinet. Anything that was not needed was in the trunk at the end of my bed. We made our beds; they had to be perfect. The matron was watching; no one wanted to get the cricket shoe for not doing their bed properly. We got into our PT clothes: white T-shirt, white shorts and socks and black plimsolls. It was time for PT.

A group of about 10 of us, my dorm buddies, met under the big tree in the front garden of the school. One of the prefects would supervise. We started off with star jumps to warm up. We then did touching the toes, sit-ups and press-ups. We did this for about 20 minutes. It did not take very long for me to get super fit. After a few weeks, I could do 100 press-ups without breaking a sweat. We would do this come rain or shine. That was how it was with all sporting activities at the school. There was never a day when it was too cold, too hot, too wet or too windy; we just got on and did it. No one complained, especially in earshot of a master. The consequences could be severe.

After PT, we returned to our dorm to put on our uniform and get ready for the day. From 7:45 to 8:30 we had prep, which was essentially like homework. This was in one of the classrooms supervised by one of the masters. Again conducted in silence. As it was my first full day I had no work to do, so I just stared at a book trying to look interested. This was boring especially for a six-year-old with a limited attention span. No one looked happy. Thank God for the bell.

At 8:30, we walked in single file and silence to the dinner hall for breakfast. I found my place, and we all stood around the tables. The masters then walked in and stood round the top table. We then recited grace in Latin. The masters sat, which was our cue to sit down also. This morning we had porridge. It was cold and disgusting, topped with cold milk. Some sugar did make it more bearable. Some of the older boys who sat at the head of the tables used to take theirs with salt. We were allowed to talk while eating thankfully. Once the plates were taken away, we sang another grace in Latin and then went to our lessons.

My first lesson was English at 9:00 a.m. The desks were very old, and I was allocated my own desk. The master was very strict, no surprises there, but he seemed fair. We would use this classroom for most of our lessons: maths, English, French, geography and history. There was about 12 of us in the Fourth Form, mostly boys of my age but also a couple of underachievers who were older. Marvin was the oldest in our class; he was 11 and had the mental age of a small child. He also used to dribble. I don't think I ever heard him speak.

This class was a steep learning curve for me. I could write basically in print and had never used a fountain pen before. Our first lesson was to practise writing letters in joined-up writing. There was no particular style taught like in state schools. We were just told to write in a way that we feel comfortable with. Unsurprisingly, my handwriting was atrocious and has made little improvement over the years. The lesson dragged, and I could not wait for lunch just to get out of there. At 12 the bell went.

We walked again in silence and single file to the dining hall for our lunch. The routine was the same: grace and waiting for the masters to sit down. Lunch was a basic meat-and-two-veg affair. The prefects would serve from the head of the tables, and we would pass the plates down the table so everyone got served. After the main course, we had a dessert, usually sponge and custard. I enjoyed it, but some of the boys turned their noses up. At 12:30 we sang grace again and then went to our next lesson.

Science! I loved science. The teacher was excellent and very friendly. We were in the main science lab. Bunsen burners on the tables and power points. I found this subject fascinating and time always flew.

At 4:00 p.m. lessons finished, and we had hobby time before dinner. Airfix models were my favourite as it was with a couple of other boys. We could also do colouring in, play with toy soldiers, stamp collecting and playing cards. This felt like freedom, and as long as we sat down, the teachers let us talk to each other. Running around was a big no. You would find yourself in Spongey's office if you did that as I learned to my cost. We could also write letters home. I used to write to my mum every week, and she would always reply. The masters used to read all letters before they were sent, or so I was told. My mum used to post me Airfix models with paint and glue. My favourites were the big battleships of WWII, HMS *Hood* and *The Bismarck*.

Wednesdays and Saturdays were different. We did classes in the morning and games in the afternoon. We did five activities: rugby, cricket, hockey, cross country and swimming.

If it was very cold and the ground was frozen, we played hockey. I hated it. We wore black shorts, red rugby jerseys and white socks with rugby boots. Our legs would turn red because of the cold. Getting a good stick was vital, as some of them had cracks, and if you hit another stick, the vibrations were really painful. The ball was lethal. It was like a big white cricket ball and just as hard; if it hit you, you knew about it. Thankfully, when it was that cold, it wasn't windy; if it had been, we would have gotten hypothermia. We also did a lot of running about, which helped keep us a bit warmer. Ninety minutes of that was enough for anyone. After the game, though, there was the reward of a hot shower – now that was nice. More often we got cold showers, so there was a little heart in the masters somewhere.

From September to Easter, it was the rugby season. This game I did enjoy though only a little. We played when the ground was soft. It was fast-moving and kept you warm. I was fairly fearless, as we were all nearly the same size as each other. There were no big bruisers in my year aged seven. One day I tackled one of the masters, who was twice my size, and was praised for it. That was my greatest moment in rugby.

In summer it was cricket. It was like hockey but more boring. I hated fielding. Standing around bored and cold in my shorts and cricket whites. Every so often, the ball would fly at you at 60 miles an hour, and you needed to be ready for it. It nearly broke my fingers a couple of times when I tried to catch the ball. Batting was far more fun; you could sit and chat with your friends, and when it was your turn, you got to try and hit the ball. For some reason, the prefects preferred fielding.

Cross country was once a fortnight as was swimming. These I enjoyed the most because I wasn't told what to do. So I did it to the best of my ability.

Cross country was a five-mile run across farmers' fields and country lanes. It took about an hour. Some of us really suffered the cold in the winter, especially the young ones. A couple of times, the prefects took boys to local houses to get warmed up by sympathetic locals. It was that bad. No masters participated in the run. We were simply counted out and counted in; that was all. There was one particular gate we had to cross that is etched in my memory. There was no easy way to cross it, and the mud was like the Somme; once we were past that though, it got better. Chilblains were common among the boys too. Luckily I never got them.

We used to take the bus to Dumfries for swimming, which made it into a little day out. It was great to get away from the confines of the school for a few hours. The bus was old, 1940s I think, and it stank of diesel, which made me feel nauseous at times. The pool was not particularly modern, but it did the job. I was one of the few who could swim before coming to the school; my mother had taught me. A couple of the boys were terrified of the water and took a lot of coaxing to get them in the pool. We were taught to doggy-paddle to start with and took it from there. The only thing I did not like was getting water in my earhole. I was advised by the older boys to jump up and down on one leg with my head tilted until it cleared. This worked every time.

Sundays were for church and hobbies. We had chapel every Sunday at 11:00 a.m. For special occasions, we went to a big church in Dumfries. Chapel was boring. The worst part was when one of the boys had to read a passage from the Bible in front of the whole school. It was terrifying. Doing this was one of my most awful memories of my whole time there. It was in my third and last year. The night before the reading, we were coached to read our passage, so we knew it by heart. So I learned my paragraphs. I walked up with relative confidence only to find I had learned the wrong passage. It was horrifying. I started to stammer and stumble over the words. I could feel the whole school staring at me. My face became red and I finally finished the passage. As a consequence, it took me years after leaving school to read in public. I found yellow paper helped, but that was in my twenties.

The best bit of Sundays was foxes and hounds. We played this in the local woods. I loved it. The prefects were the hounds, and the boys were the foxes. It was basically a big game of hide and seek. It was great fun.

We had hobby rooms where we could meet mostly unsupervised on Sunday afternoons. It was good, but I missed television, *Star Trek* and *Voyage to the Bottom of the Sea*. We were fed this line that television was for babies. I got the feeling that they did not like us being contaminated by the outside world. Everything was about structure. On one particular day, there was an old TV in one of the rooms we were using. No one was around, so I decided to see if I could get it going. In the process, I got an electric shock and a burn on my left hand. News travelled fast, and everyone knew. One of the masters commented, 'Had any shocks recently, Stewart?' In this day and age, they would have been done for health and safety violations, but that was unheard of in 1974. Suffice it to say, I never tried it again.

On Sunday, we used to play war with each other. We had two gangs: the Jerrys and the Tommys. I was a Tommy. Age didn't matter in this game, and the older boys used to join in using bits of wood for machine guns and conkers for grenades. One day, when we were playing, I challenged one of the Jerrys and called him a chicken. It was Bishop. The boys all gathered round and started to chant 'Fight, fight, fight'. I was forced into it. Bishop was one of my best friends. So we had a fight. I won, if you could call it winning. I got him in a headlock and he conceded. Afterwards, he asked me why I didn't punch him in the face when I had him in the headlock. I said, 'It is because you are my friend'. That was the only fight I ever got into at school, and I always felt bad about it.

Sometimes on Sundays we were invited to the crow's nest to see the captain and his fantastic train set. If we were good, we were allowed to switch the points and request a run of a specific engine. But we were not allowed to control the trains; only the prefects had this privilege. This was great fun and seemed a world away from the reality of the school's regime.

Music was something they took very seriously too. We were played all the classics on one of those old suitcase record decks. I loved the smell of the vinyl as it came out of its anti-static sleeve and the sound of the needle at it touched down on the vinyl. The most memorable music for me was 'Beethoven's Fifth' and 'The 1812 Overture'. The passion of the master and the cannon fire was electric. We were also taught to write music and had special exercise books with music staves on them. Looking back, I learned more than I thought, as I discovered when I was song writing in 1995.

War with Master Monty was my joint favourite subject along with science. He used to read us Homer but with some ad libs to make it more appealing to young boys. We did the story of the Trojan wars and Odysseus. There were lots of

'He had his guts for garters' added in the battle passages. The school was very war orientated as the Cold War was raging. We were the next generation of British military officers. Of course they taught us Latin as well. The dorms all had military names like Trafalgar and Agincourt. All British victories.

Apart from rugby special on a Sunday night, we were allowed to watch *The Great War* in my last year with the voiceover of Laurence Olivier. It was black-and-white and quite depressing. The picture was very grainy, and everyone walked around speeded up. It was nothing like the remasters that we watch today that have been cleaned up using a computer, but it was entertaining. It did not make me want to be in the army though. Mud, horror and death were not for me. We were also given nuclear attack training. Protect and survive. We were told that there would be a four minute warning. The most likely strike area was to the west, Dumfries. We were told to brace with the blast behind us and possibly use a door for cover. It seemed a bit futile, the radiation would, probably get us in a few days anyway. The prospects looked grim.

From time to time, boys would get homesick and run away. This was the most cardinal sin you could do. The consequences were feared like the death penalty. You would be found. You would be reinstated. You would be reprimanded. You would be punished. You would be expelled. For this they got the horse crop out. Seven of the best for the poor sod who got this one. It was treated as cowardice. The record escape was two days. We used to get updates in the main hall when a boy went AWOL. Everyone was rooting for the runner. It was literally like an escape from Colditz. Lots of the boys got homesick but not me; I just battled on knowing that one day I would get out of there.

Another reason the boys wanted to run was the bad conduct mark system. If you made a minor infraction, you got a bad conduct mark. If you got six, you got the shoe. If you got three more after that, you ended up in Spongey's office again. The problem was that if a master took a dislike to you, they would make it their personal mission to give you a bad conduct mark with every excuse. This happened to me in my last year. They knew I was leaving and were on me like a rash. I had a bad time. First, I got accused of cheating in maths. I was on my 13-times table; the nearest to me in my class was on their 7-times table. I found it incredibly easy, so I decided foolishly to take the mick. I wrote my tables on the back of my maths book for a test in jest. I showed Bishop, who dobbed me in. I was sent to the headmaster's office. Then it got worse. That morning, I lent Ferguson my Wellingtons and he did not put them back properly. This was a cardinal sin in the changing rooms. I protested my innocence but was told they were my responsibility, so I should be punished. I was sent to the headmaster's office again. I knocked on the door and was told to wait. Eventually I was told to enter. Spongey sat at his desk playing with his loaded revolver.

'Well, boy, what have you done?' said Spongey. In a quiet voice I said, 'I cheated in maths and left my Wellingtons on the bench and not in their proper place in the changing rooms'.

'Do you have anything to say regarding this?'

'Yes, sir, I do. I was only joking in maths when I wrote my tables on the back of my book. I find it really easy. You can test me if you like.' Spongey replied, 'So you have learned your tables now because you are in my office'. 'That is not true!' I protested. Had I been smarter that day, I could have argued that if I was capable as Spongey suggested, then why cheat? I would probably gotten my head bitten off anyway and my hide tanned.

'And what about the Wellingtons?' said Spongey. I told him, 'Ferguson borrowed them and it was his fault!' 'But', said Spongey, 'they were your responsibility'. I knew then I was for it. I could not reason with this man and resigned myself to a hard punishment.

'Bend over, boy.' I got the shoe. It had a wooden sole and hurt like hell. I got six of the best. I ran from his office in tears of pain and ran to the library. The boys had heard what was going on and were ready to console me. They had prepared a chair in the reading section with several cushions for me to try and take the pain away. I had seen other boys get this treatment, but this was my first time. My friend Bishop had similar luck to me. We were both on the 'bad conduct mark' radar.

After that incident, Spongey started to take an interest in me. This was my last year. He introduced me to his daughter Lady Jane, who was six years older than me. We had an exchange where she said, 'You smell', to which I replied, 'I hate you!' It could have gone better.

Spongey pulled me into his office again. He said, 'Don't worry Stewart, you have done nothing wrong. As you know we are in a Cold War with the Russians, and we need people to fight on all fronts. I have noted that you excel at physics and have an assignment for you. Watch *Star Trek*. You will find answers there. Your codename is 'Drive System'. It is in your initials. You will know what to do when you are 25. Lady Jane will be your contact'. From then on, the school became surreal. What appeared to be a normal prep school for boys was turning into a high-tech version of Hogwarts! Things became even weirder. Lady Jane took a drama class with us. She was talking about a new science fiction TV series that was in the pipeline. It was called *Battlestar Galactica*. And she was asking us for ideas for the story. I suggested rescuing a princess from the evil overlord and swinging across a crevasse to escape the guards. Lady Jane looked shocked. She whispered to one of the prefects, 'How the hell has he seen *Star Wars*?!' It made no sense at the time but not long after I found out why.

Spongey organised a special guest science teacher for us. His name was Richard P. Feynman. He was American, and to be honest, I didn't like him. He was very harsh in the way he spoke to the class and used to quote the Bible. In class he would say, 'And the seed fell on stony ground!' But as a teacher, I have never met a more inspirational man! Feynman also showed us his tattoo. It was a '666'. He also showed us pictures of other people's tattoos of 666. At the time I did not know what it meant. I had the understanding in 1995. It was profound and also humbling.

The first lesson we had was Star Trek phasers. We were given an outline of Star Trek phaser from the Star Trek handbook and asked us to draw in it what we thought the insides would look like. This was great fun, I never forgot it. I was working with Murph doing this; he was a couple of years older than me and his dad was an actor. He added the 'crocodile unit'. Feynman took them all in for marking and seemed pleased.

Lesson two was stealth. At the time, 1974, this was top secret, but we were on the trusted list. We were asked to draw a stealth aircraft using flat panels and angles of 120 degrees. This time I aced it and came up with what became the F117a Nighthawk. News travelled fast, and it was not long before President Richard Nixon came to the school to congratulate me. When I met him, he said, 'Son, you are going to be a millionaire because we live in the free world. You are made, son', and shook my hand. I wasn't sure what was going on, but one of the older boys warned me I should not believe anything he says. Watergate followed a few weeks later.

Lesson three was teleportation. Feynman was trying to stimulate our minds. He gave us a diagram of a man drawn on tracing paper a bit like an Etch-a-Sketch with a paper slider that made the man disappear. He reappeared when you moved the slider back up again. I found this interesting but crude. It got the message across, but I thought it would be nigh on impossible so delegated it to the darkest recesses of my mind to simmer for the long term until technology reached the point that it would be possible.

Lesson four was time travel. I was sceptical about this. He called me Doubting Thomas, and soon I was to be put in my place. One Sunday afternoon, all the boys were invited to the library to watch a film. This was 1975. The film was called *FX Murder by Illusion.* As you probably know, this film was released in 1986! We watched it on DVD. Spongey said they tried to get a DVD through the time displacement device before but were unsuccessful. He said the inventor must be in the room. The inventor was me; I invented DVD in 1995. This was the only film I saw at the school, but this was a fairly regular perk for the older boys. Once I heard one of the older boys talking about a character called MacLeod. The only reference I was familiar with was the detective drama of the same name. Years later, I realised they were talking about the film *Highlander.* Another film I know they saw was *Star Wars,* released in 1977. This again fell into place years later. I was unusual in that I did not see *Star Wars* until the mid-1980s. I refused to watch it, as it was not *Star Trek*, which I considered to be the superior-quality science fiction and probably because Spongey had Star Trek plans for me. When I finally watched *Star Wars,* it made me think. It was a different ideology. A galactic community either with the Empire or the Republic. This changed everything. There was another future path, not as perfect as *Star Trek* or as morally inspiring, but human, good versus evil. At the time, I supported *Star Trek,* but my involvement in the time war would change this.

***

The last few months at St Ninians were a roller-coaster ride. Several events took place. There was the chicken pox outbreak. Everyone was in bed with it. It swept the school like the plague. A couple of the boys appeared to be unaffected and were moved to another dorm to avoid contracting it. Bishop was one of them. In the middle of the night, I got up and went to the room Bishop and another boy were staying in and breathed on him. This was my revenge for the maths test incident. Two days later, Bishop got the pox. I felt avenged. But unfortunately, he got it really bad. His pocks were huge, and he was in a bad way. I started to feel guilty about it but decided he would have got it anyway.

The school play this year was a production of *HMS Pinafore.* I was too young for this, but the boys had other plans for me. Each house was to put on a comic routine and a poem reading. I got thrust into the limelight. I got a poem to read called 'Has Anyone Seen My Mouse?' They thought I was perfect for the role. I learned the poem and it went well. But next came the thing that would terrify me from acting ever again. It was a dance routine. I was the youngest of the dancers, and there was about 10 of us. I was lead dancer. I told the prefect that I was scared of everyone looking at me, but he told me not to worry. He said they just look at the stage in general and not at me. So I bought it. Rehearsals went well. Then came the night. We did the routine. It involved 10 boys dancing to disco music. At the end of the dance they, formed a line to leave the floor, and I was meant to trip them up as they headed for the stage exit. It went down a storm. So much so that they yelled for an encore. This is when it hit me. They were looking at me and I got scared. I lost my natural rhythm and fumbled the ending. It did not go down as well as the first effort. I was glad to be off the stage. So now I had two phobias. Reading in public and now acting in front of an audience. This would blight me for many years to come. I only started to get over it in my late 20s.

News got round the school that I was leaving at Easter 1976. Some of the boys would be sorry to see me go, especially Bishop, Ferguson and Roper. I would miss them greatly. We had been through a lot together. Teachers weren't so sentimental. In fact, they hounded me out of the door. Since the maths incident, I was the one to blame if anything happened. Wong crapped on the floor in the dorm. I got the blame. Someone forgot to flush a toilet. I got the blame. The real culprit sometimes came forward but not all the time. As a consequence, I was accruing bad conduct marks, and I had five. One more and I was for the high jump.

In the last week, there was a debate in the main hall. Four prefects and Lady Jane. The scenario: the five were in a balloon, and it was losing altitude. Through banter and propositions, they had to make arguments to stay in the balloon. The winner would be the last to be voted off. The boys would have the vote after each statement and decide who was to be bumped off. It came down to Lady Jane, who I felt had an unfair advantage because she was 15 and the prefects were 12. But that didn't stop her from winning. She was very popular among the boys. She would be in and out of my life for many years, good and bad.

The last lesson I remember was Sunday night stories with Mrs Spencer. We used to go to the study. We were read lots of stories there, and I really enjoyed it. We had Aesop's tales like 'The Fox and the Grapes'. At this time she was reading *The Hobbit.* She said, 'Young Stewart will be leaving us at the end of term, and this chapter will be particularly poignant for him'. The chapter was 'Out of the Frying Pan into the Fire'. And how true it would prove to be.

The last day was fantastic and scary. I had five bad conduct marks, and one more would land me in Spongey's office. I was packing my things and was very excited. So much so that I wet myself when I saw my parents' car pull up outside. I remember the echo of 'Saved by the bell' by one of the masters as I exited the building. This was the happiest day of my life so far and still ranks in the top five. My new life was about to begin.

Chapter 3

To cut a long story short, my father lost his job, which I why I was leaving. He had a big row with the owners of the hotel chain. They sent him to Stranraer in the middle of nowhere after being general manager of two rather distinguished hotels in city centres. He told them if they did not find him a better location, that he would quit. They did not; he quit. Good news for me but not the family. To compound this, my parents' marriage was under a lot of stress, and they were filing for divorce.

So I found myself in Blackpool living with my grandma and sister. Neither of us knew why; we were told nothing. We both went to Carr Lane primary school round the corner for a few months. It was not very nice at my Grandma's; the house was very old. It was a far cry from my grandmother's on my father's side with the gardens, the woods and the stream.

We lived on Curzon Road, Blackpool, with my grandma. The house was an old terrace. There was no central heating and no double glazing. The ground floor of the house had three rooms; the front room was cold and like a museum. We were told this was a special room for use if the Queen was visiting for tea. There were various knick-knacks in display cabinets, and it was altogether not a very inviting place to be. The stairs were to the left of this room. The main living area was the second room. It had old austere furniture and a coal fireplace. In one corner, there was Ozzy the parrot. He was evil. He must have bitten everybody in the family apart from my grandad, with whom he had a strange bond. I was scared stiff of that bird; it used to fly at me if I walked past its cage. Facing the rear, to the left was the main dining table, the fireplace and the main furniture, grandma's and grandad's chairs were to the right facing the fire. My grandad's chair was also near the TV so he could watch the racing on grandstand.

My grandad was a sickly man in his later years. He was a very heavy smoker and has smoked since he was in his teens. He used to cough up phlegm into pieces of carefully ripped newspaper and throw them in the fire. He passed away a year before we moved in with my grandma. He died in hospital with tubes sticking out of his chest draining the dark brown fluid from his lungs. He told us all at his bedside never to smoke, as this is what it does to you. Some of us listened.

The back room of the house was an extension to the kitchen. There was always something cooking, but the cuisine was very wartime Britain. It felt like we were still on rations. Practically everything was boiled and steam filled the air. The backdoor led to the yard where my grandad grew his roses, and at the bottom was the outside toilet and a gate leading to dog shit alley. You don't need much imagination to visualise this.

Upstairs was colder than downstairs. There was a bathroom at the top of the stairs. This was quite a luxury. My grandparents were one of the first in the street to have one fitted. There were two bedrooms. The back bedroom was where I used to sleep under many warm layers of blankets. This room was usually ready for my older cousins. The front bedroom was where my grandma slept. Some nights, when it was cold and we were frightened, we used to get into bed with grandma.

The street itself was like the old credits to *Coronation Street*: cats on walls, terraced houses and cobble streets. The rag-and-bone man used to come with his horse and cart once a week. My grandad was always ready with his shovel for any horse manure fate might send his way for the roses. We also had visits from the knife man. The milk man came every morning.

In earlier years when we stayed there, I remember running errands for Grandad to the corner shop. It was usually 10 Woodbines, a Blackpool Gazette and a grocery of some type. I remember having to recite the list all the way to the shop so I didn't forget anything. He very seldom bought us sweets.

My grandma was a very avid reader, and she had lots of books and magazines for us to read. She also had comic books about war for my older cousin Martin, who would go on to join the army as his father, my uncle, had. The stories in *Eagle* were a bit far-fetched. There was one about this soldier who could not die who was always leaping on grenades to save his comrades. I took that with a large pinch of salt. The first proper book I read was *Tom Sawyer*. My grandma had all the children's classics. She was also very clever. On the face of her, she was an old lady with a pink rinse, but she was very sharp. Her favourite pastime was bingo in the local bingo hall. Everybody knew her and it made me proud to be with her and she was jammy; she won quite often.

The most memorable people on the street were the Rileys. They had a larger corner house a few doors up. They were dirty and there were lots of them. I think they were devout Catholics, hence the large number of children. Martina was the oldest and very bossy, but we still used to play with them. They were always catching wasps which used to frequent their house for some reason. They used suspended jam jars with a jam-and-water mix in the bottom. The wasp would fly in and drown as it could not climb or fly out, or that was the theory. It appeared to work.

My sister and I made friends with quite a few of the street children. It was 1976, and the hot weather had begun. We would go walking for miles in our group and only return when we were hungry. Quite a few times, the locals would go out looking for us because it was after 5:00 p.m. At the time, we did not realise the stress we were putting my grandma under.

***

Carr Lane School was prefabricated just after the war. There were also quite a few houses in the neighbourhood that were prefab; they should have been pulled down years ago, but there was no money in the local economy to replace them.

We were at Carr Lane for only a couple of months. It was a big shock to me. I was literally years ahead of the other children; it was like the Stone Age! In all subjects, I was at least two years ahead of the local kids, and my accent did not help me integrate. I had a very posh voice from St Ninians, and the locals used to call me posh, but I was tough and got on with it. Just before the summer holidays of 1976, my sister and I moved again, and we moved back in with our mother. She had a house in Poulton Le Fylde, and it was a nice modern three-bed semi. We then started Moor Park School. This too was a prefab building. It was a 10-minute walk to the school through a park where we used to play. I liked Moor Park and made some good friends. Our teacher, Mrs Correy, was very nice and taught us nearly everything: maths, English, music and history. The class was quite small; I think there were about 20 of us but still a lot more than I had been used to. No surprise I was the brainy one in the class. Mrs Correy built a computer out of cardboard boxes; I had to sit in it as I was the computer. Classmates would write a problem onto a piece of paper and post it through a slot in the front. I would read it, then post a written answer in the out slot. The questions were really basic stuff, which I found highly amusing, but I kept it to myself. I sailed through year one of the 11-plus syllabus and I was doing very well. Grammar school, when I left, was a given.

There were two games I loved to play at Moor Park: marbles and chest fights. Marbles here was like a science. They had names for every conceivable type. Dobber, ekky bute dobber, steely and some bizarre rules like bomber and stamps. Bomber you dropped a marble into the target area, and stamps you could stamp on an opponent's marble. Chest fights, we literally clashed our chests like elephant seals, which was pointless, but they respected me, as I used to take on the biggest opponents.

The summer of 1976 was long, hot and memorable mainly for the unrelenting heat. I got burned a few times, as I have very light skin. The worse thing for me that year was my hay fever. It was hell. The standard antihistamines available then were useless. I tried eye drops and nasal sprays but none of them worked. It used to make me angry and frustrated, as I could do nothing about it. I asked my mother for the injections but was told to stop being a drama queen, as it was 'only' hay fever.

I stayed at Moor Park until the summer of 1977. At school, we watched the Viking probe land on Mars and celebrated the Silver Jubilee.

In July 1977, my mother called me and my sister into the living room for a chat. She asked us, as it was clear that my parents were no longer together, whom we would prefer to live with. Mum or Dad? It was an easy question, I said Dad, my sister said Mum. So it was settled. At the end of summer term 1977, I moved to Bolton with my father.

Since moving to Blackpool, I had not seen very much of my father. He was working in Kirkby, Liverpool, now running a 100-room Crest Hotel. It was a bit of a dive compared to the classy hotels he had run in the past. But there were things to love and to hate about the place. The first thing I noticed was the barbed wire and anti-vandal grease at the base of the flag poles. Why? They would steal anything in Kirkby. What a second-hand flag was worth on the estate I have no idea. Also, the residents' cars were frequently stolen. To stop this, a steel gate was erected at the entrance of the car park to prevent this from happening. It lasted 48 hours. In the early hours of the morning, a wrecking crew came with a tow truck and removed the gate.

On the upside, we had some very interesting guests. The Liverpool football team would drink there after home matches. One of the barmaids was sister to Phil Thompson, which is why they used to come to us. It was also quiet, and the team were unlikely to be bothered by fans. Bob Carolgeese of the Spit the Dog fame used to drink there on a Sunday afternoon. I met him once when he had Charley the Monkey with him, but I never saw the dog, only on *Tiswas.* One of my idols, John Cleese, came to stay that summer. He invited me to have dinner with him in the restaurant, but I could not stop giggling. He took offence and moved his meal to another table to carry on eating. I did not follow him thankfully. My father came by and asked why I was not eating with Mr Cleese. I just blushed and looked embarrassed.

It was in Liverpool that I learned how to write songs. Two of my father's staff whose names I have long forgotten gave me an intensive five-day song writing course. I didn't ask for it; they insisted I would find it useful in later life. At the end of the five days, when they were satisfied I was capable of writing hit songs, they tried to get me to sign a contract. Me being stubborn, I refused. It was something I learned from St Ninians. I should have read it thoroughly, but I was cynical for a nine-year-old and all contracts were probably a con. In the future, I wrote a lot of hit songs but never made a penny. I wonder if it was because I refused to sign that contract.

I loved my time with my father. He used to let me watch anything I wanted on the television. My mum's friend in Blackpool, Ann, was like Hitler with the TV. If anything good was on like *Space 1999* she would turn over and put cricket on or *Trouping the Colour*. I don't think she enjoyed any of these programmes; I think she just did it out of spite!

***

I moved to Bolton with my father in July of 1977. He was running the Bolton Crest Hotel on Beaumont Road. This was similar to Kirkby but in a better location. Again it had 100 rooms. The hotel was in two parts, the bedroom block at the back and the main building in front of it connected by a glass corridor. We lived in an apartment on the top floor, which had three bedrooms, a bathroom, a small kitchen next to the living room and access to the flat roof on the bedroom block. To the rear of the hotel was a posh housing estate. The local kids called it the jam butty estate because the mortgages were so high all they could afford to eat were jam butties. To the right was a turnip field, and Deane High was behind it. I was very happy here, and these days were the happiest of my childhood.

In September 1977, I started Beaumont Road Primary School for my last year of primary school before my 11-plus. Our teacher was called Mr Hall, and we would occasionally have Mr Partington, who was a bit like John Noakes. He was really nice. After a few weeks, it became apparent that I was doing the same syllabus year I had just completed in Blackpool in year 3 juniors. I complained but was ignored. I also told my father, who showed absolutely no interest. So I was snookered. I complained numerous times to Mr Hall, but he just found me to be annoying.

Games/PE at this school were actually enjoyable. I hated PE especially my experiences at St Ninians. We played rounders a lot, which was great fun, and also football with both girls and boys playing. This was before most of the boys thought they would be the next Kenny Dalglish; this happened in senior school. The games were fun, and we didn't have to go out if it was raining. If it was, we played games indoors in the gym, rope climbing and jumping over things. Also off-ground tig. This was great fun. The play area to the rear of the school was a tarmac. It had different colour lines in it for different games: tennis, badminton, five-a-side football. We used this for line tig. You could only run down the lines. If you touched your foot outside the line, you were out. I was pretty good at this, as I am quite tactical. As well as line tig, we played British Bulldogs. There was a grass slope to the side of the school where we played. This was good rough-and-tumble stuff, and all the boys loved it. There were a few injuries, but nobody cared in those days. 'Boys will be boys.'

Mr Hall, for all his faults, was a good teacher – misguided maybe, but still good. He used to read to the class on the odd afternoon, and he would put on different voices for each character. We also did a lot of stuff about dinosaurs. We had a discussion about mass extinction. All the normal kids thought it was a shift in climate that occurred naturally. I told Mr Hall it was a meteor. Hall was dismissive and said, 'Where did it hit then?' I pointed to the Florida basin. I was right. I can't remember if I figured it out myself or was taught this at St Ninians, but it did leave an impression. I also told them that Pluto was not a planet, and there were more objects out there like Pluto. I was about 30 years ahead of them. Feynman was probably at the bottom of that.

The fateful day arrived and I was about to sit my 11-plus. I was worried. I had done the same year twice and as bad luck had it; it mostly concentrated on the year I missed. I was hopeful but my hopes were dashed. Mr Hall was very sarcastic about this. '"I've done it before," you said! So why did you fail?' Even at age 11 I knew not to waste my breath with this man. My cards were marked. I was going to Deane High, and that was the end of it. I had my heart set on grammar school and believed I was finished and on the scrap heap now. Thankfully I was very wrong about Deane High.

***

Life in the hotel was great. I had access to all areas and got on well with all the staff. I made good friends with quite a few of them. About six staff lived in; they were down the other end of the corridor where our flat was.

Paul, the chef, used to play chess with me regularly. Neil used to mess about with me, and I caught him with his girlfriend once. He told me he had a bad chest and would not let me in. This was a standing joke for a few years. I also played Monopoly quite often with one of the receptionists.

My routine on a school day started at 7:00 a.m. I would go downstairs and go out in the staff car with one of the night porters, David. We would go and pick up some of the day staff. Their radio was particularly good in those days, lots of Billy Joel and Nazareth. David was an expert on UFOs and the kinds of things that young boys find fascinating. We had many chats about aliens and flying saucers. I loved it. I kept trying to invite him to dinner, but my father was very much against it. After picking up the staff, I went to the kitchen to see Doris for my breakfast. It was always the same: two sausages, two eggs and poached tomatoes with a mug of tea. I was set for the day.

Deane High was literally a five-minute walk from the hotel. There were two ways to get there: across a field, which was quickest, or up a road on the estate where I would meet my on-off friend, John. We would then walk the last 300 yards together. The school was in two parts: the grammar section and the high school section. They were linked by a bridge below where the sixth form was situated.

In the first year, we were in the mixing pot. Based on how we did at primary school, they began streaming us into sets. I was in the top set for everything. There were a few of us who should have clearly passed the 11-plus but did not for one reason or another: my good friends, the two Michelles,

Stuart and Rooky. The teaching was to a very high standard and was on a par with what the grammar school was delivering. I was happier knowing this but was still not fully convinced. I saw failing the 11-plus as a mark of failure. I had very high aspirations. The high school was very keen on keeping us as we made the exam pass marks look really good. And it reflected on the school. My favourite teachers were Mr Macmillan, maths; Mr Fisk, English and French; Mr Molyneux, science; Mrs Armitage, history; and Mr Hart, art (he had the same name as the TV artist Tony Hart and looked like him too). I enjoyed most of my lessons except English and French. I did well by ordinary standards, but my reports were always the same: 'David tries hard but could do better'. There was another reason why I did not try my best: bullying. I would have been a prime target if I did my best, so I ducked down to avoid being in the firing line.

My least favourite activity was games. Football was a joke: 18 boys all fighting over a ball and four of us who didn't give a damn standing around watching the melee. These boys were deluded, all thinking they would be the next great footballer. I played rugby well, as I was taught this at St Ninians, but did not enjoy it though it was better than football. I really enjoyed swimming. I was the fastest swimmer in my class and could swim farther holding my breath than any of the others. I wanted to join the swimming team, but Mr Hencher refused to let me unless I joined the rugby team. I was just as stubborn, so it never happened.

The school was in an ethnic area, and there were a lot of Asians, about 30%. There were two types: integrators and excluders. The integrators got on with everyone regardless of their religion or country of origin. Then there were the excluders, who refused to integrate. They hung around in small groups speaking in other languages and not mixing. They were mostly in the more remedial classes. I was lucky at Deane; I got on with nearly everybody, bullies and nerds alike. My best friend was Rooky. He lived on Hunger Hill with his parents Pat and Mick. They were lovely people. I would have Rooky over for dinner at the hotel a couple of times a week. We usually had steak and chips, as it was easy for the chefs to do when it was busy. I would visit his house too. His mother was very funny, and the favourite dish she served was spaghetti bolognaise. They used to watch me eat, as I found it embarrassing sucking up the spaghetti. Rooky's dad was an engineer, and he would follow in his father's footsteps. Pat was to become famous a few years later. She played Hyacinth Bucket in the sitcom *Keeping up Appearances.*

***

For reasons unknown to me, my father decided I needed a new coat for school. Everyone had a snorkel, and that is what I expected. I was wrong. My dad bought me a blue mac. I hated it and refused to wear it. Also, every time I did wear it, a bird would crap on me; this happened three times. I told my dad I wanted to be like everyone else, but he would not listen to me, so I tried a new tactic and asked one of the receptionists to have a word. It worked! No more mac and a nice new snorkel. I was a happy boy again.

In Bolton, I started to see more of my grandparents in York. My father would take me there quite regularly, and I loved it. Andre, my grandfather, was a young boy's dream grandad. He was French and came over in the war. He was a navigator on Lancasters. He escaped occupied France and crossed the Pyrenees to Spain. He was given the choice of prison or go to England and fight the Germans. So he came to England. He stayed with my grandparents Joyce and Dennis. When Dennis died in 1974, Andre came over to England and started a relationship with my grandma Joyce. Andre was an inventor and engineer. He owned several houses in France and had high-end model shops for big kids. Remote-control aircraft and the like and expensive toys. He was also a hi-fi buff and loved TV. His equipment was top of the line for its day. Bang and Olafson TV, Tandberg 10.5-inch reel-to-reel tape deck, B and O laser arm turntable, and top-of-the-range Sony tape decks. The house was fully wired for sound, and he had a designated area at the end of the living room for all his gear. I never used to touch it out of respect. He would also give me small gifts from his shop. I particularly liked kites, and he gave me some really interesting ones; it was particularly windy in Bolton. The best one he gave me was a box kite. If you have never tried one, they are particularly stable even in strong winds. I did want a Peter Powell stunt kite; they were all the rage at the time, but they were too expensive. He also used to get me things for my Hornby train set and Scalextric. I loved Scalextric, as it was a game of skill unlike the rival TCR which stayed glued to the track no matter how fast the car went. He was also a wiz with electronics and would repair my Scalextric transformer when the diodes would blow. He was a great grandad but he hated girls; he had no time at all for my sister.

The Bolton Crest was a hot bed for famous visitors and politicians. While I was there, I did not realise the significance of the people I met. Back then, the only famous people or what I would perceived as famous were Shawaddywaddy. I thought artists and politicians were boring. I saw Shawaddywaddy a couple of times; they used to do a UK tour every year and always came to us if they were playing Bolton. They were friendly and accessible people and didn't make stupid demands. A couple of them had big American cars, and I sometimes offered to clean them for an exorbitant fee. I has them down as daft enough to pay it.

In 1979, three days before the general election, Margaret Thatcher came to visit. At the time, I did not know what was happening. Phone engineers had been in and installed a multitude of phones; some of them were loud speaking phones with push buttons that I had only seen on television in our flat. The top floor was being guarded by Special Branch, who I got to meet in my father's office the day before she arrived. I was staying in one of the hotel rooms, not the flat, and it was out of bounds. I did not know until the evening that she arrived that Margaret Thatcher was staying with us. Being curious, I tried to go up to the flat to see if I could meet her. I got turned back at the top of the stairs. So plan B, I went up in the service elevator, which was adjacent to the flat's front door. This time, my timing was perfect, and she was on her way out. She knew who I was and shook my hand with a dominating overhand shake. She spoke to me and said, 'Are you the little boy who wants his flat back?' I nodded and said, 'Yes'. She then left with her entourage.

I also had a visit from James Cameron, I did not know who or what he was. I had come up with an idea for a film after seeing a picture of Arnold Schwarzenegger. I thought he would make an awesome killer android. I came up with the real skin on a metal frame, Sara Connor and the soldier from the future. The basic plot to *The Terminator*. The rest as they say is history.

The following year, 1980, the Americans got in on the act. Senator Bill Clinton came to stay; I think it was something to do with the stealth plane I helped design. He came across as a very friendly and kind man. He bought me an encyclopaedia called *Space Technology,* which he apparently took ages to find. It was a fantastic book, and it covered space flight from Goddard's and von Braun's beginnings to the space shuttle, which at that time had not yet flown into space. I loved it. The artwork was excellent, and it was an absorbing read for me, a budding aerospace engineer. It was then that I got the rocket bug. A representative from Northrop was with them. They were working on a new stealth bomber. He wanted my input. He asked me how this plane should look. I said I had no idea. He pushed it with me and said, 'Just draw something!' The drawing I did was the B2. I hit the nail on the head. The man went away happy.

That year, a couple of other interesting people came to stay: Andy Warhol and Edward Heath. I did not know who Warhol was; I knew he was an artist because one of the staff told me, but I had no idea how respected he was. I spoke to him briefly during his stay. He told me, 'Everyone is famous for 15 minutes'. I know now that that was his most famous observation, but it stuck with me to this day. Why he was in Bolton, your guess is as good as mine.

Edward Heath stayed with us for a couple of days on business. He was a friendly man, and I got to talk to him in the bar. We talked about what I was doing at school and what I wanted to be when I grew up. He gave me his autograph.

Reece and Mitchell also came to visit me. They were both astronauts. Reece was in her thirties and very attractive with long brown hair and penetrating green eyes. She had the figure of a model. Mitchell was weird. He had a sort of haze around him, so I could not figure out what he looked like. They were the crew of Discovery 2. Discovery 2 was from the future and was built on the moon. I think it was the 22nd century but I am not sure. They came to visit me for two reasons. The first was because I solved the hyperdrive equation (in 1995), and second, they liked me and would like me to go with them on a space adventure when I was old enough. I was told that flat out, the ship did 700 times the speed of light and was a long cigar shape, totally black. There was a drop ship in the hold, but I was not allowed to see it because it used technology that is classified to me. For short-stop visits they used the ship's teleportation, which did the job and did not attract as much attention.

The last notable visitor was Blake. I later found out that he was an android from Mars 2. He came to show me an electronic gizmo. It consisted of a couple of magnets, some wire and a nine-volt battery. It was a basic teleport device. He let me have a play with it, and I used it to transport a Lego brick. I did this a few times then I tried cutting the power before the transport was complete. The brick in question had a corner missing. I kept that brick for years. Blake told me that this was possible because of a theory I will come up with in 1995. He did not give me any further information and said I needed to find my own way, but I would see him again.

When Blake left, I had a go at making another one of these devices using things in my room. I had suitable magnets, wire and the nine-volt battery. And with beginner's luck, it worked! I then decided to take it to pieces and build a better one. My father would have said, 'If it works, don't fix it'. I learned this the hard way. I could not get it to work again. After a few days, I lost interest and moved on to other things.

***

That summer, my father decided to take me out of school for a couple of weeks. We were going to Bahrain to visit some of his friends. They had a son my age called James, and I was looking forward to meeting him. We flew from Heathrow, and the night before the flight, we arrived in London to stay with friends. We got to London around midnight and went for food. I asked for steak and chips but was too tried to eat it. We then went to their house, which was right next to a railway line. As the trains passed, the house would rumble and shake. I did not get a good night's sleep.

We arrived at the airport in good time. We were flying on an old DC10. It was not very comfortable for an eight-hour flight. It was noisy and smelly. I got the window seat though, which made up for it. I managed to get some sleep on the plane.

I knew it was going to be hot but not this hot. As we disembarked, I was hit by a wall of heat. It was far hotter than the hottest days of 1976! I was in for a hard time. My dad's girlfriend Ros came to pick us up at the airport in a Land Rover and drove us to where we were staying with Peggy, Hector and James. The house was a bungalow and did not have air-conditioning; there were fans on the ceilings. Inside it was a cool 85 degrees. As an act of friendship, I bought James a premium model of a Ferrari. I thought he would love it. I had high hopes that we would become good friends.

But James was a psycho! He smashed the model car up. It cost me nearly £20, half of my spending money. He was a nutjob. I could see him in borstal in the next few years. He had no respect or common sense. He was an idiot.

Hector worked for an oxygen company and showed us round his small plant. One of the by-products was dry ice. It looked great in a glass of Coke. Hector took us to see the island. Bahrain was run by a sheik. It was a dictatorship, but at the time I did not know this. Westerners were always treated with respect, as we brought skills to the island they desperately needed. There were many lucrative contracts there. A few big modern hotels and then the lesser well-off populous.

Hector also owned a boat, which was awesome. The best fun I had there was on the boat. The water was like warm bath water, and the water was crystal clear. There were fantastic colourful fish, and it was not too deep. I also liked the boat, as it was cooler there than on the island. The boat also had an observation tower to look for sharks. There were some in the area, but they were reassuringly rare. I was given a broom handle and told if a shark came near to hit it on the nose with the broom handle and the shark would swim away.

I also had a go at water skiing although not very successful, as it was a mono ski, which I am told is harder to master. I also had a go at pearl diving. Hector told me I was wasting my time, as nobody ever found one. After bringing up over 120 oysters, I found a pearl the size of a small pea. Hector asked me if he could have it. I said yes.

In the evenings on the island, we went to the Brit club. It was full of expats and contractors. I got my fix of Coca-Cola and a Mars bar. That was enough to keep me happy. They also had an old one-armed bandit. One evening, there were two guys who had been playing it all night and not won a penny. They decided to let me have a go. To their horror I won the jackpot second spin! Twenty-five dinars, which is around £30. I bought everyone a drink.

While we were on land, I constantly moaned about the heat much to my father's annoyance. One day, we went to the

Turkish Castle. Even my father complained about the heat here, which made me feel a bit better.

As it came close to going home, my father asked me if I would like to stay and extra week and fly home on Concorde. I turned it down; I had had enough. I also thought that I would never hear the end of it from my sister. She would probably have demanded a horse as compensation.

As we left for the airport, I was not sad to be leaving. I had a good time but also a bad time. It gave me a lot to talk about though. We boarded the plane and set off home to Blighty. The return journey was a nightmare. I had earache from the moment we set off until we were on final approach to land at Heathrow. That was the most unpleasant flying experience I ever had.

I returned to school with tales of my exploits. I said I hated it there, but I had to admit a lot of it was good fun. While I was away, in term time I missed nothing. I was a straight-A student, so the teachers gave the others catch-up time while I was away.

Chapter 4

It was 1980, and I was about to discover that I had a knack for writing songs. I was spurred on by two more visitors to the hotel: Mutt Lange and Reg Presley. They were both very influential in the music business at that time. They were guests, and I think one of the staff mentioned in passing that I wrote lyrics. In those days, I used to churn them out. My father called me the 'Gestetna', which was an old-style printing machine they used at the hotel for printing menus en masse. It could churn them out as fast as you could wind the handle. I had a lot of support from the staff as well but not from my father. He frowned upon this. In the end, he made me throw my lyrics in the bin, but not until . . .

Reg gave me some lessons and pointers while Mutt saw my potential. Mutt thought I would be a great lyricist for a new rock band from Sheffield. They had just released their first album, and the second was on the way. It was the third one where I made an impact. The album was called *Pyromania*. I never envisaged my work as rock, but Mutt saw it straightaway. I wrote the song lyrics for 'Photograph', 'Rock Rock', 'Foolin' and 'Action Not Words'. I never heard anything more from this until 1983 when it was released. I had no idea of the success it would be. Music press described it as the definitive rock album of all time. Quite an accolade.

Even though I wrote for this album, it is still one of my all-time favourites to listen to.

Another notable song was 'Video Killed the Radio Star'. Staff got a band together for this called the Buggles, as they used to call me bugglelugs. It was the first song ever played on MTV. Nobody ever believed me about this, and I lost touch with the staff who set the ball rolling. I wrote the song from memories about my future. My torture session in 1996, when Deb got a camera in the room, when Evil Dave got me. It will make more sense later in this book.

In all fairness, I should have been paid for this. Maybe if my father had been supportive rather than dismissive about the whole thing, things would have been different. Essentially he made me throw my talent down the toilet. If I started to write again, he would not be best pleased. The next time I wrote anything would be 1983. This was of a very different nature.

***

In August 1980, it was time to move on again. My father had been offered a new-build in Gloucester, which was a big leg up from the Bolton Crest. This was the hardest move I ever did. I was settled, I had good friends, school was going really well and I loved living at the hotel. The staff all liked me too, and I would miss them all. I pleaded with my father to stay in Bolton for another two and half years so I could finish my O levels, but he would not budge. As far as he was concerned, a school was just a school, and that was the end of the matter. Sadly he was wrong.

The school I ended up in Gloucester was called Hucclecote Secondary Modern; basically it was rubbish bin full of students failed by the system. I started in September, and my father came with me to the school to meet my new headmaster. I discovered to my horror that they only did CSEs, not O levels. Apparently their highest-performing student got five grade 1 CSE's. This was pathetic. The headmaster also said that he did not expect anyone to surpass this. My father did not care, as he said; to his mind, a school was just a school. So then we had to go shopping for a school uniform.

The shop was expensive. On the list, there were things called 'daps'. We had no idea what daps were and had to ask. They were plimsolls for PE. Also I needed white socks. There were no proper boys' socks available that day, so my father got me girls' socks! I got the feeling that a theme was going on here. So I complained again and got the standard reply of 'You will bloody wear them'.

No I bloody won't! I used to get bullied as it was without adding fuel to the fire with these socks. My life would have been hell if I had worn them. I also needed a new school bag. I was expecting a knapsack. I had seen lots of other children with them, but my hopes were dashed. I got a leather business case/bag instead. I hated it, but as I had no other bag, I had to use it. I discovered that it did make a good weapon though. It had steel sliders at the bottom, and if you slid it across the floor at someone they got out of the way.

The hotel and our accommodation was not ready yet, so we stayed a few miles outside Gloucester in Tewksbury, at the Royal Hop Pole Hotel. My dad would drive us to the new hotel in the morning, and I would walk to school from there.

My first day in the bin, I got my timetable from the headmaster's office and then went to my first lesson, maths. I sat next to a lad called Jason. I discovered his nickname was Cabbage and for good reason. He told me that I was finished at this school and had no future. Not the most inspiring first day. The maths was very easy, and I had done all this in the first year at Deane. This was now third year. The maths teacher gave me some homework; it was quite a request, and I estimated it would take a good three or four hours to complete, but I got on with it to make a good impression. The next day came, and I went to maths with my homework and gave it to the teacher. He was shocked to say the least. Apparently I only needed to do one exercise. I had done the work for the whole term in one go. The class started whispering; I was now the head brain box having deposed an annoying lad by the name of Chris Small, or 'skidder' as he was known.

Chris Small was revolting. He was arrogant, smarmy and obnoxious. He had one friend, more sidekick than friend, and was used to being the brainy one in the class. I had deposed him, and he was not too happy. If it was me, I would have been relieved, as now he was not prime target for the bullies. I had been lucky at Deane with the bullies; they all knew me and left me alone. Now I was the new boy and had to start making friends again.

On the whole, the children at Hucclecote were friendly, and I made friends quickly. My main friend was James. We played chess together and used to get up to boyish things. There was also boring Graham, who lived with his father and used to talk about the slow cooker they had all the time. His father was a TV repairman and collected old flintlock pistols and U.S. police badges. On reflection, he was an interesting man. There was also the field gang who used to hang around a field between the estate and the hotel.

This time, we did not live in, and the company bought a house for the manager and his family. It was about 10 minutes' walk from the hotel and was on a corner. As a consequence, the garden was quite large and needed a lot of mowing. To add to that, my father had the vegetable patch turfed over to lower maintenance. I got the job of mowing the grass. I used to get terrible hay fever, so I hated doing this. My father went out to Argos and came back with the smallest and cheapest hover mower he could get his hands on. I was not impressed. He told me he nearly got me a strimmer to do the job but changed his mind at the last minute. He never had any sympathy for my hay fever or anything else for that matter. He could be a heartless man at times, but I still loved him very much and respected him.

The hotel was very modern. The building was in a T shape, the bedroom block being the top of the T and the bottom of the T had the main building with the bar, restaurant, meeting rooms and kitchens. It was very well thought out. The hotel was three-star although it would have been four if we did room service. My father always said it was a pain in the neck, as it meant the kitchen had to be open 24 hours a day. My father had a few extras added in while the building work was being completed: We had a proper tape deck fitted to the PA system, so we could play anything for background music rather than the now-very-dated musac. He also had a video link system installed in all the bedrooms attached to a video recorder in one of the small offices so we could show films in the evenings for the guests. It was quite an innovation at the time. This went down very well with the guests; we would show the film nightly at 8:00 p.m. I got the job of picking the films. My favourite ones from that time were the original *Dawn of the Dead* and *Hawk the Slayer.*

The entire staff team were handpicked, as this was a major development. The hotel cost two million pounds to build, and it had to be a success. The company were gambling on my father's skills as a general manger to make the hotel work, but he knew what he was doing. The receptionists were all stunning and looked more like cabin crew than hotel receptionists. The head chef, Ray, came with us from Bolton. He was excellent and did a superior menu for a three-star hotel. He would often get compliments from the customers. He did two menus for dinner, the basic Table de Hote and the Al a Carte. The Al a Carte was different every day and of the highest quality. My father did ask his head receptionist from Bolton to come to Gloucester, but she changed her mind at the last minute. He was not best pleased. Out of all the staff, thick Nick was the funniest. The restaurant manager and I used to wind him up, saying that the hotel was being run by the mafia. He believed us. One day, I went in to the kitchen, and Nick had a bandage on his right index finger. I asked him what he had done, and he said he accidentally burnt his finger with the fryer. The truth of the matter was that he put his finger in the fryer to see if the oil was hot. Genius. Although Nick was in his mid-twenties, he had the mental age of a 14-year-old boy. He eventually got sacked for incompetence. To get his own back, he got some friends to form a band; they were called 'Mark Stewart and the Mafia', who were infamous but not particularly successful.

The main business competition for us was the hotel where they used to film the TV soap *Crossroads*. It was a few miles away. We got on well with them. If we were overbooked, we would send customers to them and vice versa. The busiest times we had were during the Cheltenham Gold Cup festival. A lot of money came to Gloucester over that weekend.

Come hell or high water, my father never ever gave me a lift to school. He even sent me to school on a bank holiday once. I insisted it was bank holiday, but he still forced me to go to school. I returned 45 minutes later. He was nonplussed.

Although the level of academia at Hucclecote was poor, most of the lessons were very interesting. The metal work teacher, Mr McGever, was excellent at his job and raised the bar with our projects. We made hacksaws and cast solid aluminium handles for them. Mine was so good that I used it when I was contracting on the aircraft. Mrs Hall taught history; until that time I had no real interest in history, but we were doing 20th-century history, which was a completely different matter. Much better than the stuffy feudal system and the Magna Carta. We did World War I and II in great detail and also the Great Depression. I left just as we started the Vietnam War. Mrs Hall was a lovely lady, and we got on really well. She told my father that I needed to get out of this school, or my education would suffer. He told me if I wanted to change schools, I would need to arrange it myself. Mrs Hall was not pleased by my father's lack of interest, so I invited her to dinner at the hotel. If I had been 10 years older, it would have been a date. We had a riveting conversation and excellent food.

The worst lesson we had was careers with a man whose name I forget. He was very overweight and had skinny legs. His opener was 'None of you will ever amount to anything. You will get menial jobs and none of you will be rich'. I don't know if this was reverse psychology, but it made me angry. How could you tell this to a class of 13- to 14-year-olds that their lives were over and that they had no hope of a successful life? To my horror, the entire class were all resigned to this. He gave us interview tips like get your haircut but about two weeks before your interview so it didn't look like you got it done for the interview. We had one lad, Stevo, who did nothing at school. He would leave with no qualifications. He said he was going to work with his dad and thus didn't need qualifications. His dad fired him. Another lad got the nickname Tramp, as that is what the careers teacher said he would become. But he was probably right.

All the boys went to the same barber, Gus Fox. He was in his 60s with a strong Irish accent, and his hands used to shake. The waiting room was full of those fold-up travel chairs, and the room was festooned with homemade pottery ashtrays that looked like a five-year-old did them. He also played this awful Irish radio station while working. His opening line was always the same. 'Is that a skinhead you'll be wanting?' I would say, 'Short back and sides, please'. Everyone got cut by Fox; he usually got you on your ear because of his hands shaking. My friends and I used to compare notes on injuries sustained during the haircut. It was because of this that I decided that I wanted long hair. And it would remain long until I was 30.

We spent 18 months in Gloucester; it was Easter 1982. My father's start up with the hotel was a success, and it was now ready to be taken over by a less experienced manager. We were moving to Wales. My only knowledge of Wales was *Ivor the Engine* and that annoying Gladis Pew from the sitcom *Hi Di Hi.* I would miss Gloucester more than I thought; the people there were lovely, but I would not miss the school.

***

Our first night, we went straight to the new hotel. We were in the car heading to the city centre. The first memorable thing I saw was a man lying in a pool of blood at a bus stop. *Is this what Wales will be like?* I wondered.

We were a family together for the first time in eight years. My sister was with us, my mum and my mum's long-term friend from Blackpool, Pat. I liked Pat; it was nice for us to be together, as now I had my mum to back me up when my father was being a nark. I had mixed feelings about my sister; she had just become a teenager and was about to go through an adolescent change, for the worst. We did family things again, and on a Sunday, we would all have lunch together at the hotel. My sister always tried to get out of it so she could spent more time with her friends. My father made her come, but I think in the end he gave up. In the end, he would despair of her.

Crest had bought the hotel as a money-losing project, and it was my father's job to turn the business around. It was in the centre of Cardiff. The hotel was 10 stories high and had a view inside Cardiff Arms Park from the top floor although you could only see half the pitch. It was a four-star hotel, which was unusual for a Crest business model, and had large banqueting facilities. There were two bars: the ground-floor bar, which was frequented by people attending events in the city, and an upstairs bar for the residents, which was open all night. It was not uncommon for the fruit machines to be stolen on very busy nights. When I first heard this, I thought it was a joke. Then, on a busy night when Wales were playing at the Arms Park, it happened. A group of about eight men literally lifted it up and carried it outside, where they smashed it up and took the money.

It is here that I got my first proper paid job as a kitchen porter. It was hard work and I worked nights to make extra money on weekends. My shift on a Saturday night started at 12 midnight; it was my job to clean the banqueting kitchen after a banquet. This took eight hours and was hard work. I cleaned everything up to the ceiling. I listened to music all night to help it go quicker. I would brush the floors first then do the first mop. I would then wash the walls and the fridge doors and oven casings. I then did the surfaces and finally the floors again to finish. It was a remarkably satisfying job. We even won an award for cleanest kitchen in Cardiff for my efforts which Ray the head chef kept in his office. Ray was a lazy bugger and delegated practically everything. While we were working, he would be smoking and on the phone to his bookie. Occasionally he would come out of his office to shout at someone. He had a knack for making waitresses cry.

***

I had high hopes for a better school, and I got one. It was a comprehensive called Bryn Cellynog. It was the biggest school I had ever been to and had over 1,000 pupils. It was built in the 1960s and had the look of a bad tower block of the period although it was only four floors. The school was in a village called Beddau, and it was rough. In fact, the whole area was quite rough. It was a bit like Kirkby; if it wasn't nailed down, it would get stolen, and if it was nailed down, they would come back with the tools to take it. Beddau was also a mining town, and the local economy relied on it. This was at the start of the miner strikes.

We lived about a mile and a half from the school in Upper Church Village, which was literally up a steep hill. This was the posh bit. The house was a new build on a new estate and was very middle-class executive. What we did not know was that at the bottom of the hill was a sprawling council estate called the Cyfadra estate, which had a reputation for violence, drug taking and hepatitis B. We were horrified. Fortunately, with us being at the top of the hill, it was unlikely that people would be walking past on their way back from the pub, but we still had to be very careful.

The school had a free bus service, and my sister and I would catch the bus at the bottom of the hill to get to school. The busses were old and rickety, but it was better than walking. The number of students was quite an eye-opener: Hucclecote only had about 300. I was worried that because of the area the school would be filled with underachievers. I was wrong. Far from it, the students wanted to learn and work their way out of this place, which was exactly what I wanted to do.

On my first day, I was given tests to check my learning ability, and considering I did 18 months in Gloucester doing nothing, I still did rather well. I was in the top sets for practically everything apart from chemistry, which I had fallen too far behind on. I was put in the CSE class. It was a struggle for me. I was a good year behind and was at the end of my fourth year. Next year, I would be doing my O levels. I had missed a lot of work in maths and physics, but they were my best subjects, so it wasn't as bad as it could have been.

The other students were very nice, and I made a lot of geeky friends. We were in gangs or cliques, and everyone looked out for each other. They were good people. There were a couple of fights at the school that the teachers tried their best to break up, but they were very violent, and this scared me. I had not seen fights like this before; they were banging seven bells out of each other. The worst of it was yet to come. The current fifth year were due to leave in July. My friend Mark advised me to either take a sickie or make myself scarce on this day. The students had a propensity for violence on their last day. In the past, they had burned staff cars and thrown petrol bombs! This year, they were being escorted off the premises by the police. Nothing major happened that day, thankfully.

My sister and I started off well and made new friends. I had a gang of geeks, which would change, and she had a gang of nice girls, but that would change also.

***

Roller boots were the in thing in the mid-80s. My sister asked for them for Christmas and became part of a roller boot gang. They were nice girls and lived on a nice estate 15 minutes' walk from where we lived. Her main friend was Laura. She was lovely and the same age as my sister. Their relationship went very well for about a year, and then it happened. My sister went through a change, and things would never be the same again for her and us, her family.

It started when she turned 14. She stopped hanging around with Laura and the others and started seeing this girl called Alison. By this time, she was a smoker and used to play truant from school. In the morning, she would pack her school bag with jeans and trainers and go to meet Alison. They used to spend their time on the Cyfadra estate 'hanging out'. Her behaviour at home became worse and worse. We never knew why. One minute, she was a respectable young girl; the next, she was a skinheads floozy. Things got so bad that we sent her to live with her cousins in Leyland Lancashire. They put up with her for a few months and then sent her to stay with our other cousins in Birmingham. This worked a little better, as Joanne was a couple of years older than my sister and could relate to her. This went on for a couple of years. My sister finished school with no qualifications. She then moved back home.

I made a good start at Bryn Cellenog. I made friends easily, and to my surprise, the geeks ruled the roost. They were all aware that the geeks would rule the world and were ahead of their time with this mantra. Each morning would start with registration. A girl a year older than me used to sit next to me. She had opted to step back a year to catch up, something I later wished I had done. All the girls took a shine to me for some reason, and it wasn't long before they were dropping at my feet. This made me very picky to the point that some of the boys thought I was gay for turning girls down.

My new friends were all going places unlike Hucclecote where nobody had a future. Most of my friends were computer geeks. I had a ZX Spectrum, Darren had an Oric 1, Russel had a Dragon 32 and the rest had Vic Commodores, Kelvin and Jonathan. Russel was a couple of years older than me and lived on the Cyfadra estate. He was *Dr Who* mad and had *Dr Who* posters and memorabilia all over his bedroom. This was Russel T. Davis, who, years later, would reimagine *Dr Who* for the 21st century and turn it into a global success.

Darren was the most entrepreneurial of us all and had a very adult demeanour for a teenager. I always knew he would go far. Darren started a software company called Compsoft, and I was one of his programmers for the ZX Spectrum. I enjoyed doing this. My programmes were fairly simple, written in Basic, but they were presentable. I wrote three games, Super Fruit, a slot machine game; X Bomber, where you bombed a city flat with a small aircraft; and Worm, where you collected flowers for points. Darren wrote for the Oric. We did actually sell some games to Finland; they wanted about 100 copies of my games. I think I got about 10p per game sold. I did this for a few months and then lost interest.

Mark lived in Beddau. It was a grotty village and a bit scary after dark. Mark had an Activision video game machine. This made my Atari look crap although they did not have as many games. I loved playing that with him. Mark was treated with electronic gizmos; I got a 50cc motorbike for my 16th birthday.

On my 16th birthday, my parents gave me a box with keys in it and told me to look in the garage. There was an immaculate Suzuki X1 50cc in blue. I was taken aback. I never expected this. I also got an Alien 2 crash helmet and a Belstaff jacket with leather gloves. I also got waterproofs.

My first day with the bike was a Saturday, 15 January. My parents paid for a Star Rider course to get me started. Pat, my mum's friend, rode the bike to Caerphilly to the training centre, which was a basically a hut and a carpark with cones to drive around. There were about six of us, and happily I wasn't the worst of the bunch. We spent about three hours doing basic exercises. Stopping and starting, riding round cones and imaginary road situations such as junctions. The three hours was gone in a flash, and it was time to drive the five miles home. I was terrified. I had to go down the A470 where everyone speeds. The fastest my 50 would go was 37 miles an hour. The ride home was hair-raising, but motorbikes started to grow on me. It was instant kudos at school turning up on a bike. There were about a half a dozen of us with 50s. After school, we used to meet up and go on little rides. I called our gang 'Vulture Squadron'. Often we would ride into Pontypridd in the evening and hang out in an underground carpark which we just used to call the 'Underground'. We were a hardy bunch and went out in all weathers.

Vulture Squadron had a rival gang, the Mods. On the roads, we were bitter enemies and would provoke each other. One of the best ones was roundabout racing. Scooters have less ground clearance than motorbikes so they can't bank as low. Consequently, they used to fall off trying to keep up with us. No one got hurt, only a few minor bruises and a graze here and there. It was funny watching the scooters hit the tarmac. They used to break up into three components: the tank, the seat and the main frame. Ironically, we all drank in the same pub, and there was never any trouble. We got along fine.

Things were going well, and nothing of note had happened for a while until Ronald Reagan came to visit me to discuss the Star Wars project and my contribution from 1995 – the future, in other words. As a gesture of good will, they asked me to choose one of two girlfriends: Heather or Mary. I picked Mary, and Reagan introduced her to me. We got on well and shared a sense of humour. Mary would pop in and out of my life, I think she found me intriguing and a little mysterious. At the time I was 16 and she was 15. I was not allowed to discuss her. This relationship was top secret although I could not see why. I had my first proper kiss with Mary and will never forget it. She was and still is a beautiful girl/woman.

Chapter 5

It was just after the time I met Mary that I read *1984* by George Orwell. This book had a profound effect on me. I realised that Big Brother was not as fictional as I first imagined. There were people that could literally get away with murder because of who they are. It was a scary revelation. I decided that I would write my own interpretation of *1984*. It was called *Operation Mindcrime*. It was a story about a drug addict who became a hitman for the mysterious Doctor X. It was about the changes Nikki went through as he became more and more trapped. The finale was a Russian roulette face-off between Nikki and Doctor X. Nikki was my nickname for the son of the devil. The final passage of the last track, 'Eyes of a Stranger', had 'You shall be avenged' played backwards. Personally I did not think it was that good and swore I would avoid it if it ever was released. I made up a band to perform this and called them Queensryche. I gave them two album titles to get started: *Rage for Order* and *The Warning*. The material was collected, and that was the last I saw of it for five years. Meanwhile . . .

In February 1983, Steve, a lad from the Cyfadra estate, invited me down to listen to a new album. It was called *Pyromania* by Def Leppard. As soon as they started singing, I recognised my work. The opening track was 'Rock Rock'. It was originally called 'Shop Shop', but I changed it to 'rock' so it didn't sound too silly. The next track was 'Photograph'. This is one of my favourite songs I wrote along with 'Video Killed the Radio Star' by Buggles and 'Eyes of a Stranger' by Queensryche. Steve was gobsmacked. We then got on to side two, and we listened to 'Foolin', which is about aliens, and 'Action Not Words', which was just about teen attitude.

Steve was convinced. But it didn't make me any richer. People were happy to take my work, but they refused to pay me. There was a simmering anger in me because of this, but in a way it was my own fault. 'They' asked me when I gave them the manuscript for *Mindcrime*, 'Do you want to be a professional songwriter?' I told them no; I wanted to be a scientist. He told me, 'You will never be rich'. Maybe if my father had been more supportive of my song writing skills, I would have become a successful credited songwriter.

Back at school, I was getting ready for my O levels. I had a lot of catching up to do because of school changes, but I did my best. I missed quite a lot of the maths syllabus and decided to wing it, as I was good at maths anyway. I wanted an 'A' in maths, but I resigned myself to a 'B'. English I hated anyway and would be happy with a 'C'. With physics I took a gamble. I got a tiny little study guide to O level physics. It was excellent. I worked through the past papers in preparation and noted that magnetism had not come up for a number of years. I knew if I got this wrong I would fail, that is, get lower than a 'C', but I was sure of myself. Metal work and tec drawing I excelled at, so there were no worries there.

August arrived and I got my results. Maths C, which I was a bit disappointed about. English C, which I didn't care about. Tec drawing, metal work and physics, all A's. My plan paid off. I also got D's in English lit and sociology. And three CSE's, maths, chemistry and arithmetic, all grade 1s. I had the results I needed for my A levels. I opted for maths, pure and applied, physics and tec drawing. This would commence in September 1983.

During the gap between my exams and results, I got my first proper girlfriend, Judy. Her friend June went out with my friend Mark. This lasted about eight weeks. I think she liked me because I had a motorbike. It made me a cool geek. We used to babysit together for her sister, who described me as a randy-looking bugger. It was the other way around; Judy was more randy than me. She was mad about babies, which made me nervous as she was only 14. My father warned me to be very careful. When June and Mark broke up, I followed suit and ended it with Judy. I saw Judy about two years later. She got her wish; she was a mother at 16.

The motorbikes introduced me to more people. I met a lad called Frank. It was the summer of 1983. Frank had a dirt bike and used it on the fields behind where he lived in Church Village. It was frowned upon, but police were never involved. Frank tempted me with the dark side and I fell. He introduced me to cannabis. I had never taken drugs in my life, and I was very anti-drugs. But he was persistent and pushy. He told me things like it is not addictive, it is not harmful, it does not give you a hangover. So stupid Stewart tried it. It hit me like a ton of bricks. I felt sick, lightheaded, but happy. If I had any sense, I would have walked away then and there and never have anything to do with him again, but I didn't to my cost. The worst aspect of smoking cannabis was that it started me smoking cigarettes, something that I was also very anti. I was hooked with the cigarettes; it took me 10 years to give up.

Frank had lived in Church Village since he was young, so he knew a lot of people. He introduced me to Ian, whose nickname was Dopey. He was far from dopey; he was one of the cleverest people I ever met. There was also Mike and Doug, brothers. Mike, aka 'Druggy', was a year older than me, and was a bit of a local legend. He was given the nickname by classmates when the teacher accused him of taking drugs because his work was poor. In fact, 'Druggy' never touched a drug in his life. He was also the lead singer in a local rock band called Singapore, later known as Teachers Pet. His girlfriend was called Mandy, and everyone fancied her. They were going places and had a makeover and an image consultant. I offered to help them with their song writing, but they declined. My lyrics were hot in those days; it was their biggest mistake. They got a Scandinavian tour, but it was not successful, so they had to get proper jobs.

Druggy had a white Yamaha RD80LC, and I had a blue one. My father saw us together on the road once and described us as 'exhibitionist' and was not impressed. He soon moved up to an RD350LC. This was the must-have bike for the young test passers. He took me on the back once; it was the fastest acceleration I had ever experienced, and it was fantastic. I passed my test about a year later but ran out of funds, mostly spent on cigarettes, cannabis and alcohol. So I never got an RD350. Frank got a brand-new Suzuki RG250 MK1, and my friend Leon got a Yamaha RD350YPVS. Leon was one of the biggest bullshitters I ever met. He had top speed claims of 135 mph on his YPVS. A tuned one could do about 125 mph in track conditions. I must admit I was a bit jealous; all I could afford was an old Suzuki X7 250. I bought it from my friend. He had bought it and then taken it to bits for reasons unknown. Suffice to say, it came in boxes.

My cannabis use really started in the summer of 1983, and I smoked a lot of it. I loved relaxing with a joint listening to music. It never gave me a hangover, and it was relatively cheap, cheaper than beer. This began to affect my school work. I was studying maths, pure and applied; physics; and tec drawing. The cannabis affected my memory. I thought I would be able to blag my way through like I did with my O levels, but I could not.

In January 1984, there was a party for me at the Beechtree social club. Frank, then my best friend, told me this party was on, and it was for me. I was a bit confused. It was not my birthday. But there were some very interesting people there. Isaac Asimov was there, and I spent most of the evening chatting with him. He was a very interesting man, and we had a fantastic conversation. We talked about Star Trek and decided that it was time to bring the show back. That night, we designed the NCC 1701 D and came up with a list of specifications for the ship: Warp 9.9, uprated phasers and photon torpedoes. Also, the ship was to stretch when going into warp. We discussed how powerful the new ship would be and that it would be massive compared to the original ship. Mr Asimov told me he had contacts in Hollywood and would get the ball rolling for a new show, Star Trek: The Next Generation. I would add more to this in 1986, a year before the show went on air.

Also that night, Lady Jane was hiding in a cupboard! She asked me to dance, but I would not. She then took me into the cupboard, and we had sex. I was only 17. She insisted over the years that I was her son's father, and she would visit me over the years. The relationship had ups and downs, but she was always true to her word.

Lastly, my father was there with some of his friends. This was odd; I knew it was my father wearing his Royal Stewart kilt, but for some reason I saw him as a stranger. They challenged me to come up with a keyboard riff, and they would make a song out of it. The riff was 'Take on Me', later performed by A-ha. For some reason, song writing was never taken seriously by my family and friends. I don't know why. With the right guidance, I could have been very successful. My mother used to say that you don't need to be rich to be successful, but to my mind, it is preferable.

The party ended, and I walked home. We never discussed the party ever again.

***

In the meantime, unknown to me, my mother had filled out an application form for the ATA (Aerospace Technical Academy) for an apprenticeship in aerospace engineering.

One morning, I got a letter saying I had been selected for interview in London. All expenses paid by the ATA. I thought, what the hell, school was going nowhere. So I went. I was given a return train ticket to London and directions to ATA Whitehall. The building was exactly as I imagined, having seen it on films. I had never been through proper security before and found it exciting.

I was directed to a sort of classroom with about 40 other hopefuls. We had one desk each. On the desk, there was a multi-choice questionnaire and some wire, pliers and a metal washer. The questions were simple logic tests. The wire was the tricky bit. You had to follow the instructions to the letter. I was confident and found it easy, but I was aware they were interviewing 3,000 possible candidates. I left the test upbeat but did not think I would get the apprenticeship.

Five weeks later, I received a letter. I had been successful! The pressure was now off, and I had a vocation. I got the last laugh at school in applied maths. We were given a complex numbers assignment. We had to read the instructions and then attempt the exercise. So I did as I was told. We handed our work in for marking. The next lesson, the teacher said, 'All of you apart from Mr Stewart have failed the assignment. This is because Mr Stewart asked his father to do his homework'. I protested, but the teacher did not believe me that I did it myself. At that point I had enough. I said to the class, 'I don't need this bullshit. I have a job which I start in September. Goodbye!' And so I left school in July 1984.

1984 was a good year. My parents had bought a pub in Chepstow and spent the weekends there, so the house was always empty. My sister was living with my cousins, so Frank, Stuart, Paul and I used to get drunk on Pat's homemade wine at the house. We were very careful, but it was guaranteed that someone would spill a drink. I would then panic and get the Jif out, which then took the dye out of the carpet. To hide it, we would move the furniture. Not a brilliant strategy because as soon as my parents returned on Sunday night, the first question was 'Why has the furniture been moved?'

The house went up for sale in the summer of 1984. This worked well as I started at the ATA on 3 September at RAF St Athan. By this time, my sister had moved back with my parents from my cousins to the pub. My parents were a whit's end with what to do with her. So it was decided that they would send her to a young ladies' college, as she had got through school without a single qualification. This did not go too well. After the first term, my parents were called to the school, and they requested that they withdraw my sister before they expelled her. So my sister went back to her life of hanging out with bikers.

My father had found my digs in Beddau with Janet, an old girlfriend. She was nice enough but had strict rules about the kitchen. I used to drive her mad. She did not mind me coming in late; she'd let me take drinks from the Tantalus as long as I replaced them. All she asked was that after eating breakfast I was to wash my bowl and spoon and then put them away. I always used to leave them on the drainer.

Looking back, it was a small ask, and I don't know why I didn't do it. Other than that, we got on OK. I lived there for about a year.

There was a works bus that picked us up and took us to work. It stopped at the end of my road. I did not know this at first, so I went on my bike the first day. I was told to report to the Picketston hangar. I had a temporary pass and had to report to the guard room first. They took ID and pictures for my proper pass to access the camp. St Athan was big. There was East Camp and West Camp as well as Picketston, where we were based. They serviced a variety of aircraft: Tornados, Phantoms, Victors and Harriers. Harriers were the odd ones out; they were serviced only by RAF personnel at that time. There were also workshops. They could literally make anything there. Only big castings or machining would be done off site with Rolls Royce or British Aerospace. This place was a car and motorbike modification heaven. You could do any tuning you wanted, and it was quietly encouraged by the instructors.

Once we had our IDs sorted, we were sent to our training camp ATA. It was on an outcrop of the base. The security there was far more lax. We were in the second of a group of three hangars. There were classrooms attached and a couple of porta cabins. I remember being watched by the other entries when I arrived. I was in 5 Tec; there were five of us. There was also Craft 13 Entry, another five. We would be trained together. The difference between the two was 5 Tec did Levels 3, 4 and 5 in college while Craft did Levels 1, 2 and 3. Also, Craft spent more time on the shop floor learning more hand skills while Tec did more paperwork. After the first year I asked to be downgraded to craft as I hated doing paper work. I was now in 13 Entry.

We went to the annex where we met our new boss, Mr Hart, who introduced himself and some of the instructors we would be having. They were all ex-RAF or ex–Ministry of Defence and had retired at 55-ish after 35 years' service on a full pension and were now on a trainer's salary as well.

We were then shown round. Our hangar was quite big. We had several training aircraft. Two Jet Provost, two Gnats, a Devon, a Bulldog and a Canberra fuselage. There was also a selection of jet engines, ground equipment and piston engines on pedestals for training purposes. We also had a bench area for practicals and access to a lathe and milling machine. There was also a funny smell, hydraulic fluid, avgas and sawdust. To the far side of the hangar was a small canteen with pool tables and a snack bar. Mr Lewis's cheese-and-onion toasties were legendary. The staff offices we also on that side of the building.

After this brief induction, we were taken to the hangar next door and were shown an aircraft that was being worked on to give us a feel of the place. Then we were put in the porta cabin to get to know each other and were mostly left to our own devices. There were 10 of us. In Tec, there was myself, Tim, Paul W and Paul L and Nick. In craft, there was Martin, Kieran, Anthony, Wayne and Bill.

Tim was the oldest at 18 when he started. At first he did not like me, but in time we became friends. Paul W was one of the cleverest along with Nick although Nick told me once I was the cleverest person he had ever met. Then there was Paul L; no one liked him. He used to smell, but then so did we all! The craft bunch were Martin and Kieran, who were partners in crime; Anthony, who generally kept his head down and was very smart; Wayne, who we all called Biggles because of his unhealthy interest in all things aircraft; and Bill, who was the most gifted fitter I ever met. On the whole, we got on well. I also made a lot of friends in 12 Entry, as Frank was in 12 Entry to my surprise. There was also Viv.

We were left to our own devices most of the time, and our first six months was about health and safety. We used this time for team bonding. We were also shown training videos. The best ones were 'Doctor Fod and Miss Waywardbody'. FOD stands for 'foreign object damage'. This was a mantra of aircraft safety. Miss Waywardbody was his beautiful assistant whose clothes would fall off. Perfect for spotty teenagers. Some of the training was not as funny, 'The Man from LOX'. This was about the dangers of LOX liquid oxygen. It was presented by a man who had been badly burned, far more so than Simon Weston, who was injured during the Falklands conflict. This was very sobering and got the point across of how lethal a mix of fuel, a spark and pure oxygen is. This was the cause of NASA's Apollo 1 disaster, which killed Gus Grisson, Ed White and Roger B Chaffee.

It was on my first day that I got my first nickname. Ryland from 12 Entry called me 'Keop' from the cartoon *Battle of the Planets,* which was very popular at the time. To be fair, it was a good observation. I had the hair and the facial features, but I could speak English!

The first instructor we had was Mr Daniels. He was in his sixties and looked a bit like Ronnie Barker. He was far from funny though. He had a monotonous voice and started every session with 'Moing', his version of 'Good morning'. Mr Daniels got me my second nickname, one that plagued me throughout my apprenticeship: 'Jack Shit'. I got it for wearing a leather jacket with a cartoon on the back taken from the *Blood Runners* cartoon in *Performance Bikes* magazine. The picture was the character Jack Shit on his bike with the caption, 'Who is Jack Shit?' Daniels took extreme insult from this, comparing it to wearing a swastika, which I thought was way over the top. A quiet word would have sufficed. From there on, my cards were marked, unfairly. My classmates would agree. This became very evident at the end of our first year. Prizes were given to the two best pupils. Nick got the first prize. Even he said it was unfair and shared the prize with me because he felt I should have won.

The first year was not very exciting. We weren't allowed near an aircraft until we had completed six months of safety training. We learned about ground safety and cockpit safety, for example, ejector seats. I was a little disappointed that we did not have any up-to-date aircraft; our planes were from the '60s. A Jaguar would have been good, even one with a knackered main spar.

Jack Shit stuck. Mr Hart, the boss, always called me this. To be honest, I quite liked it; it made me appear a bit scarier than I am.

The first year went quickly. It was at the end of this year that I moved out of Janet's house and to house-share with two RAF corporals in the village of Llantwit Major. Bob owned the house. It was a three-bed link house but needed a lot of work. The double glazing was a gash job, and there were no fittings at all in the kitchen. The cooker was from the 1950s. The house needed recarpeting throughout and redecorating. The bathroom was probably the best room in the house and was acceptable.

My room was the smallest in the house at the front. There was enough room for a single bed, and that is about all. The room was also cold all year round. I measured the temperature, and my room was five full degrees colder than the rest of the house. I was 18 at this time; Bob was 26. He was a nice man but very RAF-institutionalised. He used to call me 'dog breath' and sarcastically 'scintillating'. I called him Bob the knob.

My father would visit me about once a month and take me for a steak and to see how I was getting on. To be honest, I was getting depressed. It came to head at the end of year two. Bob was selling the house, and he thought it would be a good idea for me to buy it off Bob, and my father would be guarantor. I did not know what I was getting into. I was only 19, and this was a major responsibility. Finding lodgers was no problem. Nick took my old room, and Frank had the back room. It turned into a madhouse. Bill ended up on the sofa, as he had nowhere to live. The backdoor was always open, as people used to come and go. It was making me depressed. And my cannabis smoking became heavier. I did see the doctor about my depression, and he would only offer me anti-depressants if I gave up the cannabis. Stupidly I stayed on the cannabis; this was the trigger to my psychosis.

I used to spend nearly every night in the pub, the Tudor Tavern in the village. I spent nearly every penny I had on cannabis and alcohol. The gang would usually consist of myself, Sally, Martin and Chris and Ritchie from 14 Entry. Chris and Martin lived literally just round the corner from my house. Wednesday nights were special. I used to kick everyone out and spend the evening with Ritchie smoking cannabis. It was my way to blow off steam and relax. The others were very good about this and used to leave us to it.

Lady Jane paid a visit one afternoon in February 1986 to say hello. I was amazed that she even remembered me. The others were scared stiff of her and made a hasty exit when they realised who she was. We got on well. She took me for a drive in her Metro, and we had a catch-up. I went to bed that night thinking nothing of it only to find the entire British press outside the front door trying to get an interview. So I went out to confront them. I told them that Lady Jane was an old friend, that I was only an apprentice and that they should leave me alone. I must have been very persuasive because they did as I asked. After that, life went back to normal again.

Also at that time I did more Queensryche lyrics in February 1986. The title-track lyrics for *Empire*. It was a big hit. Again, I got no credits and no payment.

Mutt Lange got in touch in spring 1987. Def Leppard were working on a new album, and they wanted my input. He organised my train tickets and a day off work to see the band, who were doing demos. I had no material at that time, so I wrote some lyrics on the way down to see them on the train. The lyrics I came up with were for 'Love Bites' and 'Armageddon It'. I worked mostly with Phil Collen, the lead guitarist. He was a really nice man and fun to work with. He was also exactly on the same wavelength musically. And we came up with some really cool riffs together. Mutt insisted that I change my name because there was also another David Stewart who was a very successful musician at the time. He picked the name out of a book and told me that it was a really good one. The name he chose was Nigel Green. I hated it; I preferred Dave to Nigel, and I hated being called Dave at that time as well. I refused to do it, so he told me if I wanted to be paid, I must change my name. I didn't; I never got paid. I was angry about this, but it was my own fault. In hindsight, I should have just agreed; my friends would still call me Dai, but I did not think of that. The credit is on the album *Hysteria* and is an accurate description of me aged 20, full of conspiracy theories and wild assumptions. It was a shame. They gave the name to someone else who eventually tried to sue the band. I did not know what that was about.

***

The parties were nearly every weekend and used to drive the neighbours mad. Harry on the left was in his 70s and was partially deaf. Our concession to him was that we let him play his electric organ at 3:00 a.m. The other side we called the 'Drill Rig'. One of the lads nicked a sign with 'Drill Rig' written on it and an arrow. I put it in the living room window pointing at their house. There was a RAF guy and his wife. They hated our loud music. It came to a head one day when I deliberately made a row to annoy him. He was livid. After that, relations warmed, and we got along fine. They used to send us Christmas cards from the Drill Rig.

One Sunday afternoon, the fire brigade arrived. Apparently there had been a report of a fire at my address. Obviously it was a hoax call, but we had to go by procedure. The living room by this time was full of traffic cones, temporary diversion signs, toy guns and bongs, and there was a motorbike in the kitchen. I saw the fire engine pull up outside and went out to ask them what was going on. They told me a fire had been reported at this address and that they had to come in to make sure the house was safe. Reluctantly I agreed. I had never been so embarrassed. I could see the fireman was trying not to laugh as he entered the living room to look round. He then went into the kitchen. He left with a stifled grin on his face. Next minute, the others came in to have a look as well. I got the 'Sorry to bother you' spiel as they left in fits of laughter. After that, I had a crackdown on brining stuff back to the house when the guys were stoned.

The worst incident happened a few days before the fire brigade visit. Martin and Chris came home with a 5-by-7-foot sign in bright yellow. It was from the centre of town about some major road works that were due to start in a few weeks. I made them take it back. I used to dread the day when temporary traffic lights would be in the living room. Thankfully they were not crazy enough to try that one.

***

After several months of Daniels's monotony, we had Mr Lewis and Mr Watson. They both liked me, which was a refreshing change, and I liked them. They were good, honest people, and if they did not know the answer to something, they would find out. This was the mantra across the training school.

While I was there, I invented 'Ear' ear defenders. Those yellow rubbery things. I came up with the idea because my grandfather got a bus ticket stuck in his ear once. I thought if you got the right plastic compound, you could compress them to fit your ears and would be easy to remove. They bought me a tray of various plastics, and I picked one that I thought was suitable. They came into production quite quickly. I was never thanked or rewarded.

Mr Watson knew me from the 1960s and a time-travel incident. I was sent back in time by Northrop on North Star One, our first superluminal star ship. The ship had a teleport facility and picked me up from my flat in 2012. I was taken back to Blackpool in 1960-something. It was winter and bitterly cold. They dropped me off by an old Radio Rentals shop with a buddy. The shop was amazing; the stuff was ancient. It was absolutely fascinating. Unfortunately, we did not have time to explore. The mission was to meet my grandad and tell him about the Tornado programme. We walked to Curzon Road where they lived. I went to the door.

This was weird. I knocked, and I think it was my mother who answered the door. She must have been late teens, early 20s at the most. I told her I was from aerospace and needed to talk to Eddie about a matter of national importance. She let us in. My grandad Eddie worked at ICI but had a lot of contacts and was well respected. I shook his hand and started to explain why we were there. I told him I was sent from the future and that the Tornado Project was a go. They needed to find a RAF engineer called Bob Watson, who would pioneer the development of composite structures. I explained it would be a swing-wing multi-role aircraft with Rolls Royce triple-spool bypass engines. I think I showed him my mobile phone and my buddy showed him his digital watch as proof we were from the future. It was a very surreal experience, and that night is etched in my memory. After our chat, we said our goodbyes. I told them I would see them again in the future. I think they figured out I was related. Oddly enough, my mother mentioned it about six months before I was sent. I told her when I went but she then lost all memory of that night, or so she said.

Chapter 6

Colby became our primary instructor in 1985 and was the most interesting by far. He was in his mid-60s then, so he must have been born around 1920. He served in the World War II and had tales to tell. After we had done our curriculum work, we did all kinds of other stuff. We got involved in film-making and aircraft development, and we even got a budget from the U.S. government for an experimental aircraft which I designated as Aurora.

During the war, he was stationed in the Mediterranean area. I am not sure if he was army or air force at that time, but he was very high ranking by the end of the war. He told us about the Mitchel bombers designed by the man who designed the Spitfire. It is a lesser known story about RJ Mitchel. These planes were flying death traps. The ground crew used to 'accidentally' set them on fire so no poor bugger had to fly them, to which the air crew were eternally grateful.

In Colby's class, we were also taught stealth. This was unheard of for British students being taught stealth. We were given technical specs on the F117a Nighthawk, which had just gone into service for the U.S. Air Force. We were allowed this because I was in the class. The Americans were familiar with my file and my designs from boarding school under Feynman.

Colby did not like me very much. My attitude was very anti-establishment; I had long hair and was notably clever, all traits he did not like. Stealth is surprisingly simple when you know how it works. Getting a stealth plane to fly, though, is a different matter. That is where the genius comes in. At the time, the B2 was on the drawing board, another of my airframe designs. We asked for specs on that too but were unsurprisingly told to sod off.

We had a good link with the Americans at the school probably because there were so few of us being trained in this area. We worked on the concepts for the F22, F23 and Typhoon Eurofighter. We split into two groups. I was on the F23 concept while Nick and Paul W were on the F22. As you may know, the F22 Raptor won the contract. It was the best loss I ever had. The F23 was the most beautiful fighter aircraft ever made to that date.

Colby took the lead on the Typhoon, using technology that the Americans did not for various reasons. I won't bore you with the details, but we nailed it in class. The info went to NATO.

***

I told Colby about my meeting with James Cameron in 1979 where I came up with *Terminator*. It was a runaway success, and I wanted to make a sequel. At that time, sequels were notorious for being flops, and this was a big gamble. We got made an offer by Cameron's studio. They offered us a shoestring budget, and we had to come up with a plot. The plot was silly but clever. Someone down at bioweapons division dropped this chemical into the ocean, which kills a bacteria, which kills an amoeba, and works its way up the food chain eventually killing everything on earth. So the CIA are doing a deal with a bunch of aliens who are offering two options: the big gun or the good package. The big gun kills everyone, and the good package is the cure. Clown squad wants the big gun, and the CIA want the antidote. All the aliens ask for is a glass of water. The film was one of the most successful low-budget films ever made. It was called *Real Men.*

After this, we did some story work on *Aliens,* which went well. So we got funding for *Terminator 2*. Colby orchestrated the story using a flipchart. We decided to do the story with myself as T1000, and my friend Paul was the now-obsolete T800 played by Arnold Schwarzenegger. We put it together like a computer programme and made sure that there were no plot holes which could ruin the film. Our work got sent to James Cameron. He got back to us fairly soon after and offered us a deal. $100 million had been allocated for the film; this was the most expensive film ever made in its day. He said if we wanted in, we would be liable if the film flopped. If it was a success, we would be rewarded handsomely. Everyone got cold feet except me. I was certain it would be a massive hit. It was. The film was released in 1991 and was the in-flight movie for the troops going to Iraq for the Gulf War. I was paid in excess of £600,000. I could have taken more.

***

Star Trek: The Next Generation was now in pre-production. And we were in contact with Gene Roddenberry. I invented the Borg. They were my adolescent space nightmare. The cube ships were a show of their technological superiority. I also invented the Q Being. I got the idea from school in Bolton from John, who was half-French. He was the most condescending know-all I had ever met. He was perfect for this, and his nickname was, not surprisingly, 'Q'. Gene loved my new enemies, but he was worried about the Borg; he thought we may have overcooked it. *Next Generation* was on video next summer, 1987. The local video shop used to get them in once a fortnight. There were two episodes on each tape. The first season was brilliant. They were fantastic to watch and were a breath of fresh air for the time.

Colby was a proponent of time travel. I always regarded it as dangerous, as things have a habit of coming out of the blue and blowing up in your face. Colby had some kind of scope. It was not a physical thing, more like an ethereal presence. It permeated our classroom. I am sure he had access to a freezer like the one at boarding school, but he never let on. What I did discover was that my work from 1995 had been sent back in time. I am not sure how far it went back, but it must have at least been 1980. That would explain all the interest in me by famous people especially the Americans.

Depending where you sat in our classroom, you got special powers. I used to know things without knowing why. I knew the Israelis had nuclear weapons, but I did not know how. Looking back, it must have been caused by the time loop I was in, leaking information about the future. The computer from my ship *Discovery 3* played a part in this. It was strange.

Colby reminded me of the Emperor from *Star Wars*. There was something very sinister about him. He was a very powerful man and had a lot of contacts. He had allies in both the British and American governments. The odd thing was that Joe Public had never heard of him.

Colby excluded me from time travel, and as predicted, it blew up in his face and the class. The lads literally shit themselves. They were looking 15 years into the future. 911! Suffice to say, that was the last time they meddled with time travel. This also taught me an important lesson in time travel: things are not easily fixed if you know the outcome and want to change it. Should Colby have been held partly responsible for what happened that day, as he did not successfully prevent it from happening? My thoughts on the matter were a little like the Enigma code story in World War II. Once they cracked the code, they could not afford to let the enemy know they had done it, which resulted in the bombing of a convoy. They could have warned them, but the Nazis would have found out we had cracked Enigma. I think something similar happened with 911; there may have been a nuclear device in the mix. Who knows? Time travel is very dangerous.

I admit I had a hidden agenda. I knew that a lot of things supposedly fantasy were in fact real. For instance, hyperdrive and teleportation and now time travel and AI computers. Knowledge of the breakaway and Spongey's school helped me with this. Where I was once a sceptical young man, I was now at the sharp end of Earth's secret technologies. Interestingly looking back, I came to realise what the ATA were getting from me was a watered-down version of my work. We looked at hypersonics and FTL drives but came up with blanks. Tim got mixed up in this and was trying to sabotage everything. He thought everything was too advanced for him, and he was belligerent with the whole thing. This was rocking the wrong boat. Bill Clinton beamed into the apprentice school and grabbed Tim by the scruff of his neck and told him to 'Stop fucking with my administration!' For once, Colby was speechless.

The films I wrote screenplays for in 1995 had also gone back in time. The most notable one was *Titanic.* Colby was determined that I would never make a penny from any of my work. Because of the success of *Real Men* and *Aliens,* Colby wanted us to make a lemon to use up the money we had made. So we made *Howard the Duck*. Wayne didn't get it. He was hopeless at movie-making but believed he was a master, so we left him to it. We also pioneered Ducktronics. I found it highly amusing, but I was also mad that we were wasting all the money we had made. It seemed to me typical ATA logic. Small time and on a shoestring with no ambition to get out of it. I used to think that only America's way was right and so they would be the recipients of my work, not the

ATA. This ruffled a few feathers, and I did not give a damn. I was sick of being shoe-horned into crappy mediocrity.

Colby was very cagy about *Titanic*. He never mentioned the film, but I figured it out years later that he must have known. He was convinced that I had been on it. I denied it, but he wasn't convinced. The trick of the plot was that both Jack and his friend were time travellers, which is why they gambled for tickets to get on board. There was another trick to the film, but that is between me and James Cameron.

Because my work from 1995 was so good, they wanted me to fail. So I deliberately made a stinker. Colby started having a go at me about it because it was a flop. I figured out what I had done in the future to warn myself. The film had a band in it that I hated, which is why I used them. This was my version of *Howard the Duck*. When they found out, they panicked! I was in stitches. I knew I would booby-trap my work because people are greedy and lie about what they have achieved. I experienced this first-hand on more than one occasion. After this, I had a brief spell as God at the apprentice school. I was a nice God and very forgiving. In hindsight, I could have been harder, but I am not a vindictive person.

As well as figuring out how the Blackbird worked by myself, the instructors were always very interested in my take on things to do with aerospace, especially propulsion and airframe design. Colby did not like it and was determined to ruin me. He made it his mission to. He knew about my future career and was especially interested in my work at Dornier in the early to mid-'90s. He was angry because I landed the best job in our class. I was working on NATO military aircraft. This was my third time at Dornier. He made sure that I would not go back again. He had me tortured in a very clever way using what he called a snail gun. It would get me few years down the line. He described it as knurling.

Meanwhile, things at work were getting interesting. One afternoon, I was pulled in by the camp CO for an interview. I had no idea what it was about. Colonel Rimington was there too. This is where the story gets bizarre. I was under investigation by MI5 because I apparently destroyed an M Class star freighter. I was told that the 'company' were looking into it. Apparently there were these things called interfaces which stuck to people's eyes and were nigh on impossible to get off. They were like white plastic blindfolds without the straps. They could move like caterpillars and were intelligent; they could also reproduce. They got you when you were asleep. There was an outbreak in my underground base, so I asked Blake to set a fusion reactor to destroy the base and the interfaces. It also destroyed the star freighter.

The resulting argument would not have been out of place in a science fiction movie. To top it all off at the end of the interview Rimington said to me, 'Thank you Ripley'!

I was curious. Who are this company? Rimington told me that I started it in the 1990s. This was weird; I was being reprimanded for something that I had not done yet. They had me down for serial time-travelling. Up to that point, I had only time-travelled once. And that was in the USA in 1888 when I got the inventor of Coca-Cola to patent Coke on Friday, 13 January 1888, my birthday. It's 'the real thing', from the 1970s advertising campaign. I did this around the time I was introduced to Mary in 1983. Reagan sanctioned this.

I left that office a little confused and excited. Unbelievable things were happening to me. I knew I was part of something bigger than myself, and I knew outer space was going to be involved.

***

One sunny afternoon, I was taken to the main camp and a small parade ground. There were some green crates with things written on them such as 'Sidewinder Missile' and 'Pershing Two'. The instructors had dressed up as Arabs and other ethnic groups. I was told to sell them the weapons, and they played the interested parties. It was good fun, but it had serious undertones. I knew this was not a joke and that at some time in the future I would have to do this. The rest of the class looked on; I was becoming way out of their league and had been given an informal status as general so I could kick ass.

The last few weeks of Colby's class was war-orientated. We were aware of the collapse of the Soviet Union and knew a lot more than the man on the street about what was going on. They were also planning the first Gulf War and the war in Yugoslavia. We got our hands dirty for the first time and helped coordinate air strikes and took sides in Bosnia. Colby engineered it so that the future me would be on the other side of the conflict. I think he was hoping that 1987 would win. They did not; future me did a classic half-pincer movement, which brought a quicker end to the war and saved lives. The younger me was not happy with my future to the point that I wanted a divorce from myself. Colby must have been rubbing his hands together in glee!

Our time at the training school was coming to an end, and it was time for improver training on the shop floor for our last 18 months. This gave me insight into all of the different aspects of aircraft maintenance. We were all split up and sent to different sections. We spent three months on each section.

My first placement was the flying controls maintenance. In this section, we did repairs to flying control services, either aluminium or composite. There wasn't much composite work because the Tornado was still relatively new. I learned a lot about sheet metal working, and I knew this was what I wanted to do. I took great pride in my work and loved working to very exacting standards. Most of the craftsmen in this section were civilians. These workshops were in a row; this was 7 Squadron. I moved down the building.

Next up was the hydraulic bay. This was the most fun placement on the camp. It was mostly RAF and very easy-going. The principles were simple, but you always needed a close eye on health and safety. Radio 1 was on all the time, and the coffee breaks were long. This was a new location for the hydraulic bay, as the last one got smashed down. Two of the corporals were testing a Tornado nose leg to 3,000 psi when it exploded, knocking the shop wall down. Luckily no one was hurt, but the incident was infamous at the base. One of the older lads from 9 Entry worked there, called Ivy. He was a good laugh and liked to mess about a bit. We kept a large spider in an old fish tank and used to set up battles between the spider and prey. We started off with big flies and worked our way up to a wasp. The spider won.

Next was the tyre bay. This place was a joke. There were three staff: two chargehands and their semi-skilled fitter, Ritchie. Ritchie did all the work. A day in the life of the chargehands was 8:00 a.m.: put the kettle on and get out for the newspaper, for example, the *Daily Mirror*; 8:30 a.m.: tell Ritchie what to do; 8:30 a.m. until lunch: watch television; 12:00 p.m.: go for lunch and then play snooker until 2:00 p.m.; return to the tyre bay and wind down. To make it worse, these skiving gets were the union representatives for the camp. While I was there, I thought they would help me and I was looking forward to working with them. I was having problems at the school because some of the instructors and the boss, Derek Hart, had written me off because of the Jack Shit episode. They never forgave me. I asked the reps for help, but they would not help me unless I voted Labour. I refused; I was a Thatcher follower. Had I had more sense, I should have either lied or gone to a solicitor claiming discrimination. There was a big kick-off regarding this. While I was on 7 Squadron, a high-ranking ATA officer visited the bay and asked me to do something for him. He was very pleased with my attitude and quality of work and asked me which section I would like to work on at the end of my training. I told him they were letting me go because I 'did not fit in'. He was very angry and went to talk to Don Graham, Mr Hart's boss. I don't know what was said, but nothing came of it.

After 7 Squadron, I went to work on the aircraft. I spent three months on the Victors, mostly up a wobbly set of steps trying to fit power flying control units. I hated it; I didn't like heights, and those things were very heavy. The guys I was working with weren't bothered; they reminded me of those men from New York who built the Empire State building without safety lines and eating their lunch on a metal girder 300 feet in the air. The best part was ground-running the Victor. The noise was incredible. Wearing ear defenders, you could feel the sound resonating in your chest. It felt quite nice actually, but you did get the feel of how much power these planes could generate. On one of the runs, they asked me if I wanted to do a cabin pressure test with the pilots. I said yes. It wasn't very pleasant. It was a recipe for bad earache. I forgot about the Bahrain incident on the way home. Had I remembered this at the time, I would have said no. The pressure built quite quickly, and I could feel my ears popping. Next, water squirted out of the side of my eye. Thankfully none of this hurt, but I was relieved to be out of there.

After the Victors, I did a stint on the Tornados. This was a biker's dream. Tornados used titanium nuts and bolts, which were great for replacing the ordinary steel ones on most Japanese bikes. Ninety per cent of my time on Tornados was spent aligning the flaps. This was a nightmare. There were four on each wing, and they had to line up exactly with each other when the flaps were up and down. It sounds easy, but it was the hardest job I ever did on an aircraft. It took us literally weeks to do one aircraft. I was glad to be out of there.

The rest of my training was on the tools. The fabrication shop was the best, but you had to stand most of the day. It was here that one-off bespoke components were made. The guys on this section were highly skilled. They had tools here I had never seen before: rubber presses, shrinkers and stretchers and wheels. The parts were made from templates using the old component as a guide. I really enjoyed this, and I learned more here than anywhere else on the camp. I was sorry to go. My last placement was on the other side of the camp. To be honest, this section was a joke. I was designated a man called Bert, who was probably the most boring man I ever met. All he was interested in was horse racing. His job, if you could call it that, was to refurbish 12 identical components in 12 months. One a month. He ran through it with me. I could have done one at a leisurely pace in two days, and that was stretching it. I could not believe that someone could have such an easy job. This was taxpayers' money.

The last year at the school we spent wrapping up in preparation to leave. At home, things were driving me mad. The parties and the drugs.

In the summer of 1987, Ritchie turned up with some LSD tabs and said we have to try them. They were apparently top grade. I refused because I was integrated on the master system, a telepathic link to 'God'. I was put on it in 1980 by Bill Clinton, and he warned me not to take drugs, as it could have severe consequences. Frank was his usual persuasive self, so I agreed. More fool me.

There were three of us in the house that day in the summer: me, Frank and Viv. We each took a tablet, and I felt fantastic and high. That was all I thought they did, so I suggested we take another one; Frank did, and Viv went upstairs to his room. About 20 minutes later, it hit me like a tonne of bricks. Everything melted; I could see sounds and time slowed down. It all started as fun; we were watching *Star Trek 2: The Wrath of Khan.* Then it started to get sinister. 'Retina eye scan for Project Genesis.' I was shitting myself; this was real! This was part of my work from 1995.

A while later, three of my friends beamed into the living room. This was heavy stuff. The trip lasted about 10 hours. I was glad when it was over. I knew it had done me severe mental damage and was the final push of my schizophrenia. From there on, I was a bit wonky and got worse. I was listening to the radio that morning of the come down; 'Don't Worry Be Happy' was playing. The drugs were the main reason I decided to leave Wales. One day, I came home to find tinfoil paraphernalia of someone who had been smoking heroin. I never found out who it was. That was the last straw. I would stay until the end of my apprenticeship and then until the house sold.

In the Christmas of 1987, Frank and I went up to Scotland to visit some of his relatives. We spent New Year's Eve in Edinburgh and then went to a little village where his parents lived. We arrived after a two-hour drive around midnight. We had a nightcap and then went to bed; I started seeing people in Victorian dresses walking around the room. I asked Frank if he could see them, and he said yes. I thought he might be winding me up and that it was caused by the LSD damage to my brain. I asked him if the house was built next to a cemetery, and he said yes. I was then sure he was pulling my leg and went to sleep. That morning, I opened the curtains to see a massive graveyard next to the house!

***

Passing-out day arrived. I was the only one there without my parents. Don Graham handed out the diploma scrolls and indentures. I was the only one in the class who was not indentured. This was a done deal, and there was nothing I could do about it. Colby had seen to that. They were expecting me to cause a scene, but I did not. I had more sense. I shook Dave Lewis's and Bob Watson's hands. They were on my side. They knew it was unfair but had to tow the party line. I was out of there! Thank God.

I spent the next few weeks partying and looking forward to leaving Wales. The others all wanted me to stay. But things were out of hand. I knew the house was under surveillance because of the drugs. We had a regular drug dealer who came to the house, and a lad called Dean used to pop up from time to time. He was a major-league car thief and used to drop stolen gear, mostly car radios, off at the house to wait for it to cool off. My love life was also a mess. I was seeing Sally while she was seeing Frank. I wanted to give them some space, which was another reason to leave.

They all tried to sabotage the sale of the house by painting a patch of the bathroom wall black and just being obstructive. Bill was the only one who helped in the end. We burned nearly everything: the sofa, beds and furniture. We took it all in a van to the local trading estate at Llandow to burn it. It was good fun. There was an old TV in there which exploded and a couple of used tins of WD40 which went off like rockets. It was sad in a way, but I needed to leave and face my own demons. Bill was kind enough to take my stuff up to Southport in a van while I led the way on my bike. He was a good friend; he ended up working at Stanstead. I tried it for a few weeks in 1990 but hated it; it brought back memories of the ATA and the ridiculous attitude on the shop floor.

To add to the story, Lady Jane came to visit me again a few times. She once turned up in the middle of the night with her bodyguards. The main bodyguard from Special Branch I used to call 'Knuckles'. They were there, as they had been following leads on Operation Julie, which disturbingly came to my door. I remember Knuckles saying, 'Shall we kill them?' 'No', Lady Jane replied. She then had a private word with me. She told me I was her sons' father because of the liaison we had at the Beech Tree party in January 1984. She said she wanted to have sex with me on a semi-regular basis when her timetable permitted. I was absolutely agog by this. She being a Lady and I being just a graduate apprentice. She told me there were rules. No telling anyone. I had no idea what she saw in me. I never had myself down as particularly handsome. My mother used to say I was, but then she was my mother! Lady Jane had big plans for me, but I had no idea what they were. They then left in the night.

The house sale went through in October. I made a tidy profit of around £3,000 and was 'loaded' for the first time in my life. My father told me to buy another property in Southport, but I declined. I was worried that there would be a rerun of the madness at Monmouth Way. My mother said it would be different this time. I was insistent. My father told me I would regret this in later life, and he was right, 20 years later.

The run-up to Southport with my stuff went without a hitch. Earlier that day, I had a meeting with Lady Jane. She had a little job for me. She showed me a cut diamond that was about the size of a big conker. She told me that diamonds of this size usually have a history of violence and murder around them. I was my job to get the diamond to Southport, and she would pick it up a couple of days later. I had a think and said it would be fine, not a problem. She asked if I was sure. I said I was and to trust me, and I knew what I was doing.

I had a good think how to transport it without losing my cool. I thought about sticking it up my bum but had a horrid vision of some drug crazed knife-wielding maniac cutting it from my backside. The option I came up with was simple but risky. I simply put it at the bottom of a cardboard box full of junk. I figured no one would look there even if they had a tip off.

It worked, and the diamond was safe at my new residence in Southport. True to her word, Lady Jane appeared, and I gave her the diamond. I had passed the first test.

Chapter 7

My father had bought a restaurant in Southport. It was on an avenue behind the Scarisbrick Hotel, a very short walk from the promenade. The avenue was lined with Victorian buildings with businesses all the way down to the promenade. On the corners were amusement arcades and the rest were chip shops, café restaurants and seaside shops. My father had a restaurant called the Victoriana. It served traditional English cuisine and was the only food outlet on the avenue that had a bar. It could seat around 40 diners and was very popular. We lived above the restaurant; the upstairs was very spacious. My father had the top floor, I had the room at the front on the second floor and my mum had a self-contained flatlet on the first floor. My room was big, and I had a phone by my bed. There was central heating, and I had a gas flame coal effect fire installed for extra heat. The floors were all bare wood, which I had carpeted. There was a good view of the avenue from my window, and you could people-watch from my window as tourists walked by.

At that time, I had a lot of money from the sale of the house, so I was in the mood for buying things. My priorities were stereo first, everything else second! Southport has lots of shops for a small seaside town, so ordinarily you don't need to go to the cities of Liverpool or Preston to buy things. To my great delight, I discovered a hi-fi shop down an alley called PA Audio. It was heaven; they were Technics dealers. They also had a listening room and loads of different makes and types of speaker systems. In one afternoon, I spent £1,000, which was a lot of money in 1988. I bought a top-of-the-range CD player, a class AA amp and Cerwin Vega speakers with a 12-inch sub-woofer the size of a coffee table. They kindly delivered for me and offered advice on setting up. It sounded awesome. My favourite thing was having a joint and listening to ultra-high-quality sound. This system nailed it. I have an eclectic music taste, so most of what I played loudly in my room was appreciated by my father and mother, who would often ask me to turn it up!

My next mission was to find a good pub, so money in pocket, leather jacket and trainers on, I went in search of the best bar for my tastes in Southport. After trying about 10 different pubs, I came across a bar called Smarties that had really cheap drinks. The barman was just the person I needed to give me the lowdown on the scene in Southport. His name was Gary, and we are still good friends to this day. He told me there was nothing in Southport regarding work opportunities. There was either the hospitality industry or the care industry. I had noticed a lot of old people in town. He asked me what I did. I told him I had just finished my apprenticeship in aerospace engineering and that I planned to go contracting in Europe. He was impressed. Gary then asked me what my favourite bands were; that is when we hit it off. We both loved rock: Def Leppard, Heart and the like. Gary told me that there was a rock club in Southport, and he would take me there and introduce me to the rock crowd. He said to meet him Saturday at the Ship for 9:00 p.m. for a couple of drinks and then we would go to Raffles.

So on Saturday we met as planned. Raffles was rock heaven. It was across the road from the station up a flight of stairs. To my surprise and delight, I knew the doormen, Mick and Gordon. They had worked for my father at the Bolton Crest in the late '70s and early '80s. They recognised me too. The main area of Raffles was the dance floor. At one end there was the bar, and at the other end the DJ booth. The floor was sticky, and the place smelled of cigarettes and alcohol. We were there early, so it was still quiet. Gary introduced me to Gary L the club owner, and his partner Micky, who had an uncanny resemblance to Blondie, and the two DJs Mike H and Andy O. Once it got busy, it really started to rock. They played a very broad range of rock. I thought I knew about music in Wales, but this was another level. They introduced me to some great bands: DAD, Steve Earl, Cinderella and Giant. I would never have heard of these if I stayed in Wales. Southport was looking good. I thought I would be happy here and I was looking forward to the future.

One thing that Raffles was really famous for was the stay-behinds. After throwing-out time at 2:00 a.m., we would lock the doors and drink, listen to music, chat and smoke. I used to get free range on the decks and loved using the equipment. I got the bug and wanted to have a go at DJing. Andy O showed me the ropes. Andy was a professional DJ who used to have shows in the midlands before moving to

Southport; Gary L had snatched him up. What Andy O did not know about rock wasn't worth knowing. He showed me how to cue records and how to mix one track into another using BPM (beats per minute). He also imparted the necessity to play to the audience. A full dance floor is always a good thing. It was here that I also met my best friends, Andy Shack, Mike S and Tim S. All three of them were DJs. Shack used to play the Ship with Andy O before Raffles on a Saturday night. Rock in those days was massive. Rock nights always got the crowds in. The main competition was the Floral Hall, which also ran a rock night every Saturday night. People preferred Raffles because it stayed open later, and there was more chance of getting more obscure music played. The Floral played mainly to the mainstream.

There were various other rock venues, as everyone was trying to cash in on it: the pub the Steam Boat and a couple of others. Champers was also popular. I had a couple of strange moments in Champers. Strangest of them all was a visit from the Skunks from Lockheed. They came into Champers wearing Lockheed uniforms and told me to follow them. They had a surprise for me. On the embankment by the Marine Lake, they had landed in a drop ship. These vehicles were capable of reaching orbit and had vertical take-off capability and stealth. It was awesome. I got to have a nosey at the state-of-the-art cockpit and was dying for a go. They asked me if I was interested in a reconnaissance mission. I was absolutely made up. Wow! I took the offer. At the time, I don't think I fully appreciated what I was letting myself in for. They told me I would be on OPS on

Pathfinder 2. I did not ask what happened to Pathfinder 1. The drop ship took me to the Skunk base where we boarded Pathfinder 2. This was a time ship, not a starship. Starships can time-travel, but dedicated time ships are better at it.

Our mission was to get through a time barrier at the start of the 23rd century. Nothing from beyond this date was coming through the freezers. Navigating this was not easy. It was a bit like mountaineering. Every so often, you needed to hammer in a peg for your safety line. The dangerous part was having to take sides in conflicts as mercenaries. The ship was very advanced and could hold its own until the 'plateau' of the 26th century. The 'plateau' is the point where technology stops advancing. It is also called the 'Deck'. This was our target.

When we got to the 23rd century, we figured out that the barrier was there because of a war in the 24th century. Pathfinder 2 was capable of penetration. We passed the 23rd without incident, as there were no major conflicts, but we became aware of what the trouble was all about. There were two main factions in the 24th century: the Republic and the Federation. It was a bit like the cold war of the 20th century but far from cold. The Republic was the Star Wars faction and the Federation was the Star Trek faction, and we had to pick a side. If we chose the Republic, we faced the Empire. If we chose the Federation, which was morally superior, the future was less certain.

It was a tough decision to make. The crew voted, and we chose the Federation. It was, we felt, the right thing to do. Doing the right thing does not win wars.

The level of death and destruction in this war was like no other. There was mass murder on both sides, although the Federation was the worst. All those mirror universe episodes told a story; in hindsight, we would have gone with the Republic. The ship was captured. The Republic were merciful. They sent us on to the Deck.

The Earth in the 26th century is beautiful. There is no war, no poverty and everyone is free. The most staggering thing I remember was the moon. It was covered in cities that were visible from a telescope. Earth was now a truly interstellar community. Business and trade were run from the moon; it was fantastic. I would love to have stayed, but we were then sent home with a mission to warn the past about the future. I dreaded going back; I knew I was in for a hard time. My life had just gone a whole lot more complicated.

They teleported me down in Southport where I left. I had been gone in local time about 10 minutes. I walked back to Champers, my head in the clouds. My dreams were coming true and so were my nightmares.

The run-up to Christmas was one of the best I ever had. I received over 100 Christmas cards from Wales including a card from Lady Jane and her partner, who I never met. I had my first social visits from celebrities this Christmas too: the Rachael's. They just turned up one day relying on their fame to get them in. Rachael and I did not hit it off; Rache was the quiet one. Rachael described my room as 'like Aladdin's cave'; I got the feeling that she was insinuating that I stole all my possessions. She knew about my work on *Terminator 2,* which at that time had not been released yet. She was berating me over this, as she 'knew' it would be a flop. They bought a film with them from the freezer, *Buffy the Vampire Slayer,* which would be released on 31 July 1992. I was convinced it would be a hit and that a TV series would go down a storm. Rachael told me if it was a flop, it would be on my head, so they called it Sand Dollar productions so they would know who to blame. They called it this because I had sand dollars in my room from my visit to Bahrain in 1979. They had not seen one before. Also, the Rachael clause, as I called it, should this be a success I was to get no credit. In short, she was a bitch.

When Rachael saw how many Christmas cards I had, she asked me if I save them every year. I told her no; they came this year. She of course did not believe me, like everything else I told her. I would get the last laugh. Rachael and Rache became bored with me and left.

We had a few visitors from Wales over that Christmas. Jack, the landlord from the Tudor Tavern in Llantwit Major, came to stay for the night on their way to Scotland. My father and Jack got on like a house on fire. I also had visits from Richie, Frank and Viv. These were good times. They all wanted me to come back to Wales, but I would not budge. Then one night at Raffles, Lady Jane came to see me.

It was a busy Saturday night when Lady Jane and her entourage came to Raffles. Everything stopped: the music, people talking, everything. She told me to go back to Wales. Everyone missed me, and they would love me to come back. Being the idiot I was, I chose to ignore her orders. In hindsight, I should have done what she said. Anyone with half a brain would not disobey a Lady. When they left, the club went back to normal like nothing had happened. No one ever mentioned it again. My downward spiral continued.

At this time, I still had a bike, a Suzuki RG125, which I loved. It had been derestricted and went like a 250. I decided to go to Wales for a couple of days and took a selection of new rock music that backwater Wales was missing out on. The first night I spent at my friend Claire's house in Church Village. I parked my bike up at the front of the house, and we went to the pub. How quickly I forgot that anything not nailed to the floor in Church Village would be stolen. So we returned after the pub to find my bike gone. I was not happy. As a result, I had to get a train home, and it ruined my visit, reinforcing why I did not want to go back to Wales.

On the upside, I still had over £3,000 in the bank and could afford another bike, so I was not too worried. I had a chat with my mum about what to do with my gap year. She said travel. My mum had friends in Canada and thought it would be good for me to visit them. The bike could wait. So I organised a one-month trip to see Chris, Cynthia and their daughters in Edmonton. I would spend two weeks with them and two weeks travelling. I booked for the first week of January. This was the first time I had ever gone abroad alone and was excited and nervous at the same time. I had always wanted to go the Americas, and this was as good a start as any. Bags packed and I was ready to go!

The winter of 1988/1989 was mild as I remember it. It was nothing to what would be in store in Canada when I got there. My dad took me to Manchester Airport in his MR2 and wished me luck.

I was flying with Canadair on a Boeing 757. The flight was quiet, as it was off season, and I had a full row of seats to myself. I was near the back of the aircraft, somewhere I would get used to being later in the year, with the cabin crew. I had a copy of Max Born's *Einstein's Theory of Relativity* for 'light reading'. The bar on the plane was free, so how could I resist? I had developed a taste for black Russian cocktails, something I was introduced to by Gary while at Smarties. (The drinks there were the cheapest in Southport.) The flight was about 11 hours. The view from the window was awesome as we crossed Greenland. You could see the mountains, glaciers and sea ice. It was a very clear day. The black Russians kept coming until the cabin crew warned me that you are not allowed to get drunk on an aircraft for flight safety reasons. I knew this and did not go over the top.

As we approached Edmonton, the captain announced the weather conditions. Dry, sunny and minus 25 degrees Centigrade. Wow. I thought, this is the coldest place I have been by a country mile. The airport was quiet, off season, compounded by the coldest temperatures in 20 years. I got through security very quickly. The lady on the passport checking desk asked me where I was staying and how long I would be in Canada. I would have happily talked to her all day. She was the most beautiful woman I had ever seen. She made Pamela Anderson look like an ugly sister. Quite a welcome.

I got to arrivals to meet Cynthia. She came on her own. Chris was working, and the girls were at school. My mum gave us both pictures, so I knew her straightaway. I found Cynthia very easy to talk to; we got along well. We went to the four-by-four, and there was snow piled up at the side of the roads. The roads were clear. We could learn a thing or two about handling heavy snow.

Everything was very colonial. Most of the private residences were part pre-fabricated wood and brick. They all had basements with the air-conditioning systems in them and under-floor heating. Chris and Cynthia's house was a bungalow with a large basement which had a spare room with en suite where I stayed. There was a picture on the wall of an aircraft trying to land in hazardous conditions, which stuck in my head. At the time I still smoked, and Chris's family were all non-smokers. It was nice of them to accommodate me, but they did try to make me give up.

I stayed with them for the first week, and we did a number of things. First, we went to Edmonton Mall. In 1989, it was the biggest mall in the world. It was fantastic. It was on three levels and as well as shops and restaurants it had a fun fair, submarines and all kinds of art installations. There were a couple of shops that appealed to me, a hi-fi shop that had the latest surround sound kit and amplifiers with ridiculous power outputs. At home 80 watts per channel was a lot, here some of them pushed 200 watts. There was also a coin and stamp shop that I found fascinating. There were old dollars from the Wild West and gold and silver coins. I was tempted, but the main thing I went to get in Canada was CDs that were unavailable in the UK. DJ Mike H requested an LP by White Sister that was impossible to get in the UK. I was after Cheap Trick albums too. Unfortunately, there were no decent record shops in the mall. We walked round for a couple of hours window-shopping and then went for something to eat. Michelle suggested a sub. I had never heard of a sub. She told me it was a sandwich in the shape of a submarine, hence the name. At the time I had never heard of Subway. Now they are everywhere.

My next little excursion was to the Edmonton museum. I knew the North Americans had little history, but this surprised me. Pre-1850, there was practically nothing. There were lots of exhibits about Native Americans, and to be honest, it was quite boring. I liked the guns though. We did American gun-making during my apprenticeship and learned how the Colt gun company invented precision engineering so all their gun parts were interchangeable.

In the evenings, I would pick films for us to watch. I was an avid film buff back then and watched practically every new release there was on video. I could not believe they had not seen *Highlander*. It had been edited, which surprised me. The scene during World War II where he finds Rachel had been edited out. Why, I do not know. They were a tough audience; they thought it was 'OK'. I also showed them *Mannequin*. They hated it, much to my surprise.

The best excursion we did was to Banff skiing. It was about a four-hour drive. Before we went, we did a little practice, as I had never been skiing before, and I took to it quite well. Banff is a small town that relies on the tourist trade. It is mostly cafes and restaurants and ski shops. Chris lent me one of his jackets, as I had nothing suitable. It was fun. The girls raced off ahead, and I got a skiing lesson. There was a group of about six of us, and I was making great progress until the instructor told me I was doing really well and I promptly skied into a tree. But it was a good day. At the end of it, we went for hot cocoa and then headed home.

Next on the agenda was Calgary. I elected to go by bus as opposed to the train because (a) it was cheaper and (b) I thought it would be more fun. Cynthia took me to the bus station. The bus station reminded me of an old airport with the TV chairs that you put coins in to watch while you waited. The bus was how I imagined a Greyhound bus to look: mostly silver with a logo down the side. It was a quiet trip, I had a couple of seats to myself, and the view was fantastic.

I arrived in Calgary in the evening and went to the first decent hotel I could find. I checked in and then went to reception to ask if there were any good bars in town. They suggested the Brass Ring bar. So I jumped in a taxi and set off to have a good night. I met a very attractive blonde in her late thirties, and we spent the night chatting and dancing. It was a great night out. Around midnight, I left to return to the hotel and had the bar call me a cab. I got in the cab, and he asked me where I wanted to go. I then realised I had forgotten the name of the hotel. I got him to take me into the city, and I was not holding out for my luck. We went past a couple of hotels, and I had visions of having to go to the police to ask them to ring round hotels to find out where I booked in. Just as I was about to give up, we passed a hotel that looked familiar. I went into the lobby; this was it. Boy, was I relieved. I tipped the cabbie and went to my room. I learned a very important lesson that evening. When staying in a hotel in a foreign country, always carry the name and number of the hotel you are staying in!

I went to my room, and it was what I would describe as exposed. It was by the stairs and near the breakfast restaurant. It made me paranoid. I started looking for hidden cameras in the room and had a very unpleasant night. To make it worse, housekeeping threw me out at 8:00 a.m. to clean the room. So I took the opportunity to go for a walk in the city. Not much was open, as it was still early, so I just had a wander around. I walked past the bus station and then decided to retrace my steps back to the hotel to see if my room was ready. There was a mass of people coming in the opposite direction that I did not notice before. They were all in their work clothes going to catch the buses to work. I was the only one going that way and felt compelled to turn round and walk back with them, so I did and felt much better for it.

I had enough of Calgary, so after just two nights, I got back on the bus and headed to Vancouver. This journey was far more interesting. I remember the awe I felt when we were approaching the Rockies. It was literally a wall of rock and was spectacular. We made a couple of stops along the way, and I got the looney who sat next to me. He told me he had just been released from prison. Actually, he was very interesting to talk to and told me stories of his habitual kleptomania that had got him behind bars on a number of occasions. He had no money; he had been put on the bus to Vancouver by the police and had to check in when he got there. I offered to buy him lunch at the next stop, but he declined.

Old habits die hard. When we got to a diner for a 20-minute break, he was stealing from the canteen. I knew he was doing it but did not see him doing it. The staff were watching him like a hawk, but he got away with it. Our next stop was Kamloops, high in the Rockies. This was like a Wild West town. Everything appeared pre-fabricated and very colonial. As we had an hour this time, I decided to go for a drink in the local tavern. To my surprise, there were pictures of Mary on the walls. The barman took me to one side. He said in the interests of my health, it would be good if I left by the backdoor. The locals are no fans of young English tourists. I took his advice and headed back to the bus. The time went quickly and then we reached the point where we finally started to go downhill. I thought we would be in Vancouver in about an hour, tops. It took four hours. The decline seemed to last forever.

When we arrived at the bus station, my new friend took me to a local hotel, which was rough. When I went in, it reminded me of the hotel that no one in their right minds would stay in. The man behind the desk gave me a lecture: no parties in the room, no drugs and no hookers. I got in the lift, which had two hookers in it. As we went up through the floors, there was the smell of drugs of various types. Quite a den of iniquity.

The room at the hotel was seedy but reasonably clean. The view was inwards and faced a square with air-conditioning units by every window. Vancouver was noticeably warmer than Edmonton, a barmy 10 degrees Celsius. I went down to the bar and thought I would try and score some cannabis. I got talking to a local, and he said he could sort me out. He said he wanted me to come with him, as he didn't want to get caught dealing in the hotel. So like an idiot, I went with him. We walked to a housing estate about 25 minutes' walk away, and he asked me to wait on a corner while he went to get the cannabis. I stood on the street corner like an idiot for 20 minutes then a police car went slowly by just as my drug dealer returned. He then, in full sight of the police, gave me the bag or cannabis. I was terrified; luckily they continued to drive past and did not realise what we were up to. I had visions of getting arrested and deported in shame. Lesson number two: when in a foreign country, do not buy drugs from someone you meet in a bar!

I headed back to the hotel feeling slightly relieved and went to the bar for a beer. After a quick drink, I headed up my room to try my illicit substance. I had smoked a lot of cannabis in my time, but this stuff was a different ball game. It was much stronger than the stuff at home; it was called Skunk, and it lived up to its name – it stank. I was off my face in no time; I spent the evening watching *Star Trek: The Next Generation.*

The next day, I went into the city exploring. I found a couple of really good record shops and got the White Sister album for Mike H. I also got some Cheap Trick albums unavailable in the UK on CD. I then headed down to the harbour and found a nice café. While I was there, I noted in a local paper that Cheap Trick were playing at the Vancouver Arena. This made the trip for me; they are my joint favourite band along with Def Leppard, but I never worked with Cheap Trick. They were playing that night, so I decided to go along and try to get a ticket on the door. It was almost a sellout, but I managed to get in on the main floor and found a spot by the mixing desks. The first act was Eddie Money, who I had vaguely heard of. I was stoned off my box and was looking forward to the music. Eddie Money blew it. He came on stage high on probably cocaine and after about 10 minutes was booed off. The guys on the mixing desk were chanting 'We told you, we told you!' It gave the night an ugly complexion, and I was regretting having smoked that joint and could not wait for it to wear off. Cheap Trick came on at 9:00 p.m. as billed and played an excellent set.

After the concert, I walked to the main road and found myself walking in the other direction to everyone else. I went past a man with a black eye patch who snarled, 'Look at it!' as he walked past. I then walked to the taxi rank. I had a long wait; it must have been a good hour before I got a taxi. I was almost relieved to be back at that dive hotel.

I spent about a week in Vancouver, and in hindsight, I would have found a better hotel and also stayed off the cannabis. But it was a major learning experience and made me a wiser man. The final day came, and I packed my bag, flushed the cannabis down the toilet and headed back to the bus station. The journey back to Edmonton was uneventful but pleasant.

I rang Cynthia as I neared Edmonton, and she was there to pick me up. In the four-by-four, I told her the edited highlights of my trip. She asked if I went to the island. I told her I did not know about it or where to go. Exploring by yourself is not as much fun as being with someone.

On the last couple of days, I cooked for the family. I went to the supermarket and got premium ingredients. I was making beef stroganoff, and I think I did a pretty good job. The girls Michelle and Annette loved it. On the last night, I took them out for a meal at a posh restaurant to thank them for putting me up. The restaurant was very pretentious, and we all found it quite funny. I ordered Scampi Provençale, but it was not what I got. I complained, and the waiter said that he did not think I would know the difference! I decided not to push it in the interest of having a relaxing night.

We said our farewells, and they dropped me off at the airport. I went home feeling enriched and that I had learned some important lessons in life as well as having an interesting time. The flight was uneventful and quiet like the journey out. I spent most of the time looking out of the window. The in-flight movie was *Gorillas in the Mist.* My dad picked me up from Manchester Airport and took me home. There were lots to talk about to my friends on my return. It was nice to be home.

I spent the next few weeks bumming around and then decided that I needed a job. I went down to the job centre for the first time in my life. In those days, there were cards in the window with the jobs and pay written on them. I picked a couple and took them to the desk. One had already gone.

The other was for a job at Steam Port by the station where ASDA is now. It was for a sheet metal worker for trains. It seemed right up my street. The pay was OK. and the contract was for three or four months. I went to the site office for my interview, which was essentially to look at some technical drawings which explained the job. It was a breeze; I got the job. This also made my father much happier. I offered him rent, but being like he was, he refused it, which I found a little annoying. Anyway, it got me out of the house, and I was doing something constructive. This was my first taste of contracting.

Chapter 8

It was a rainy, cold Monday morning, and I turned up on time with slight trepidation. This was the first proper job I had since completing my training, and I had high expectations. The men I was working with were hardened contractors, and I was the youngest by a good few years. Most of them had been recruited through an agency, I was the odd one out because I came from the local job centre. There were a few things I found a little disconcerting. They were using electric tools, not air tools. The roof was leaking, and I was scared of getting an electric shock. Also, they heated the place with gas blowers a little like mini jet engines, and lastly they talked in 'milly', not 'mill', when discussing the job ('mill' is short for millimetres).

To be honest I didn't learn much there, but the people were nice. The job mostly entailed removing screws with an impact screwdriver and drilling holes for heavy steel rivets. To use the impact screwdrivers, you needed a four-pound hammer. I ended up with a massive muscle on my right arm, it made me feel like a bit of a freak. The weeks went quickly, but I was glad to see the end of it. The working conditions were poor, nothing like in a hangar. It was time to go back to aircraft.

The first thing I needed was a toolkit. Luckily, there was a good tool shop in Southport. I got both metric and AF spanners, as I was not sure if I would be working on Boeing or Airbus. Boeing was AF and Airbus was metric. The air tools were a little harder to get. My mother was a credit controller for an air tool company, and she got me a pistol windy (hand drill).

A few of my friends from 12 Entry, the year before me, had gone out contracting, so I got in touch with Cambridge Aerotech. In those days, you could get a job merely off recommendation. There was no interview; they just asked me where I did my training and who I knew, and I was in! The only question they asked me was whether I could travel at short notice. I said yes; I was only an hour and a bit away from Manchester Airport. That was all they needed. A couple of days later, I got my first job at Schiphol Airport, Amsterdam. I was told to go to Manchester Airport and go to the KLM desk and ask for my ticket. Everything was taken care of. I was met at arrivals by the company rep who took me to Hangar 10 where I would be working. Hangar 10 was one of the biggest hangars in the world in 1989. It was massive; it could hold two 747s in one go. It was hard not to be impressed.

There I met up with Viv. It was nice to see him. We were then taken by minibus to the hotel in the heart of Amsterdam and given our per diem, which was about £240, beer tokens! Our money was in two parts. The flat rate then was £10 per hour. The per diem was tax deductible, and the rest went home. A very nice arrangement.

The hotel was a three-star just round the corner from one of the best tourist spots. It was there we discovered the T'café, the little Bulldog and, about 20 minutes' walk away, the little Hard Rock Café, which was the best of the bunch. All these bars sold cannabis, and I was happy to indulge. Most of us did. There was a good selection, and thankfully none of it was as strong as the skunk from Canada. I was comfortably numb most nights. This place was like a holiday camp.

We started work at 8:00 a.m., and the mini bus was there to take us to work. The journey took about half an hour. We were all introduced to one another and then were told what the job was. It was a 747 D Check. That is airplane talk for a major service. It was not as daunting as it sounded. The jobs were relatively simple: remove lots of screws and look for corrosion. Our team leader, Pete, looked at my tools and told me to see the storeman to get an upgrade. Gone were my Draper tools and hello Snap-On. The storeman charged me peanuts for them. I had some classy gear.

The job was easy: remove the screws from the floor boards and take them out. Then make new boards using the old ones as stencils. Each one was numbered, so you know exactly where they came from. To get the screws out, we used Snap-On speed braces. Because there were so many screws, the braces used to wear out, so we had to replace them all the time. This was free, as Snap-On have a lifetime guarantee. Cutting the boards was not so nice. I worked on this with Viv. The first time I did it, I got a rash from the fibreglass and ended up in the med centre at the airport.

They gave me some tablets and told me to stay away from fibreglass.

The tricky bit was the lap joints. Our group was brought in as specialists to do this job. I must admit I didn't have a clue, but the older guys knew what they were doing, so it wasn't that bad. Essentially it involved taking the rivets out of the nose section skin looking for corrosion between the sheets of metal. If there was corrosion, it was cut out, and a repair scheme was used. This was my first taste of heavy riveting. I learned a lot on that first job and also got a taste of decent money.

There was a canteen at KLM, but it wasn't very nice. The signature Dutch dish was Nasi Goreng, which I did not like very much. It gave me the runs. This was usually the main thing on the menu. I think even prisoners would have complained about this!

The time at KLM went quickly, and I had a great time. At that age, all I was interested in were beer, cannabis and loud rock music. The bars I went to all had mega hi-fi systems. The best was in the T'café. It was all top-of-the-range gear matched with very high-quality speakers. It was there I was introduced to Mr Big and other classic rock bands from that era.

Our favourite place though was the small Hard Rock across town. Not very many people knew it existed, and there were hardly any tourists there. They had video screens there and often played Def Leppard videos, so I was right in my element. They also had the best selection of cannabis resin in the Dam. I particularly liked Nepalese Temple Baum; the Afghan was also very good.

One day I was walking there with Viv and I got mugged. I was wearing a gold necklace my mother bought me and a gold razor blade I got from a jeweller in Chepstow on full show. Stupid! I think the razor caught the mugger's eye. He pushed me to the ground and grabbed my necklace. I thought about trying to fight him off, but he kept putting his hand in his pocket like he had a knife, so I decided not to. Everyone walked around us like we weren't there. It was most disturbing. I should never have had the gold on show.

I arrived home just before Christmas with money in my pocket and ready to party. Before I went home, I bought my mum a windmill model that played a tune when you wound the sails. She loved it. Viv came up to visit, and we spent most nights in Raffles rocking out and getting very drunk. It was heaven. Southport was a great place to be if you liked rock and wanted to party. Viv was particularly popular as he had Afghan, which is very rare in England. It was much better than the local crap.

Part of Gary L's licence required that he had to sell food to get the 2:00 a.m. licence. God knows where he got the stuff from; it was cheap and not particularly nice. They were little curries in a pot, and they tasted like cotton wool. People did not believe it until they actually tried one.

At the time I used to drink mainly black Russians, partly because I liked them and partly for image because they were expensive. As a consequence, I ran out of money quickly and needed to go back to work. Thankfully work in those days was easy to find on the aircraft.

New Year came and went, and I was back in Amsterdam. This time, things were a little different. I was on the same flight as Viv luckily. I had flown from Liverpool to Heathrow to get my Amsterdam flight. When we got to Schiphol, no one was there to meet us. Viv suggested we get the bus to Hangar 10 to find out what was happening. When we got there, the rep was waiting for us to take us to the accommodation. This is where I met Billy. Billy was an experienced contractor in his 40s. He had a friend called Bill, and they always hung around together. I liked him straightaway; he was well educated and very clever. He used to read the *Times* or the *Telegraph*. These papers were readily available in Amsterdam, as they were popular with the Dutch. You could also get BBC1 and BBC2 on television there.

We were told that we had been given alternative accommodation, as the Smit was full. Personally, I think they were just saving money. We were taken to a tower block estate called Ganzenhoef. On the way there, we were given a list of dos and don'ts: Never go out by yourself. At nights, move around in groups of four or more preferably if you have to leave the flat. Don't carry large amounts of money and keep your head down. I wondered what I had gotten myself into.

The apartment had three bedrooms. There were two beds in each. A sparse kitchen and living room with a balcony and TV. The first thing I noticed was the beds were away from the walls. I asked Viv and he did not know. That night we found out why. The place was infested with cockroaches. The beds were away from the walls to stop them climbing into our beds. The kitchen was full of them too. We complained to the rep, and he said he would get the place fumigated next day. But we realised this would only set them back a bit because the whole block was infected. We complained but were ignored.

***

Billy was the most mysterious man I had ever met. I am sure he was in some kind of secret service, be it MI5, MI6 or CIA. He knew inside information on practically any political or military project. This is when I got into my first really scary time-travel incident. Billy told me that there was a worst-case scenario for the airport. The scenario was that a passenger 747 would lose an engine on take-off from Schiphol. The plane would then be diverted to an emergency approach over the Ganzenhoef estate. It would not make it back to the runway and would hit one of the tower blocks. This of course was a secret so as not to alarm the public. It did alarm me! Someone had time-travelled, and Billy told us this awful thing was going to happen. As a general, I could request time-travel clearance to see if we could get to the cause and prevent it from happening. General Schwarzkopf gave us clearance.

We knew the airline and the aircraft. It was an Israeli 747 cargo plane. We found out that there were two of them. General Schwarzkopf got in touch with Colonel Rimington, and we arranged to intercept the aircraft at Swiss Air to do thorough checks on the engine pylons. By this time I was in a state. Being born on Friday the 13th was partly to do with it; some airlines don't have row 13. I was terrified that if I touched it, it would crash and it would be my fault. To be doubly sure, they replaced all the pylon bolts on both aircraft. The others were confident but I wasn't. I knew this plane would come back to haunt me.

***

Swiss Air was the most intensive aircraft servicing centre I had ever been to. They repaired aircraft from all over the world at very competitive prices; this attracted some really dodgy customers. It was quick and cheap but professional. I was put on the Boeing 757s. The work environment was horrible. They had a massive workforce on the aircraft getting in each other's way. I did not enjoy my time in Switzerland and was glad when it was over.

I got a job with German Cargo at Frankfurt Airport with Billy. This was a doddle. They hardly ever needed us, so we spent our time chatting and smoking and drinking coffee. The downside was that we could be needed for two days, then go home, then return 24 hours later. I did not mind.

Frankfurt Airport is next to a massive U.S. military base. On 2 August, the preparation for war in Iraq began. We watched the American Galaxy Transporters leaving Frankfurt every two minutes. I had no idea they had that many aircraft. Lady Jane turned up to say hello. While she was there, I martialled an aircraft into the hangar, as there was no ground crew available. And I did a good job if I might say so myself. She told me that my Sharp stereo I got from the Naffi at St Athan was going up with the Discovery Space Shuttle. She then left with her usual air of mystery.

As we were watching the aircraft on a clear night, I saw a ring of 12 stars in the sky to the south. I got the feeling I was the only one who could see them. Billy told me he could, but I didn't believe him. My take on it was they were military satellites deployed to scare the Iraqis. There was something biblical about this and not in a good way.

While we chatted in the workshop at German Cargo, the subject of the *Star Wars* programme came up. I was convinced it was a real thing. Billy told me it was all a bluff by the American government to bankrupt the Russians. I found out years later he was correct.

The war was getting going, and things for me were getting really exciting. Reece came to visit me at home in Southport. The giveaway technology was her Mars 2 medical laser. State of the art. It used a nanite beam laser with telepathic interface. It was mainly used for battlefield first aid, but it could be used for less serious conditions or injuries. Reece decided to give me a facelift. She stopped my ears from sticking out. They used to call me 'wingnut', among other things, in Bolton. She also modified my facial structure very subtly.

Reece wanted me to come with her on Discovery 2 to Mars 2. This is when she told me the history of Mars 2.

At the end of World War II, the Manhattan project had made far more breakthroughs than just the atom bomb. These breakthroughs were too important to go public, as they would jeopardise the safety of the Earth. These breakthroughs included hyperdrive, 666 times the speed of light, and teleportation with five-dimensional non-Euclidian geometry. They also built the world's first time displacement freezer. This is how they made the breakthroughs so fast.

The first ships were ready in the early 1970s, the Breakaway. It was decided to set up the Mars 2 base at Proxima Centauri with utmost priority. The moon landings made the ideal distraction in case any of the breakaway craft were detected, which was unlikely but still a possibility. We needed a guard dog.

Mars 2 is a sovereign state and has its own government. It is run by scientists but is very Wild West. This was the new frontier. By the 1990s, the base was big and operating with alien races. Reece wanted to show me round. How could I refuse?

Before we left, Reece had to do a projection. This was a time scope. You could look into the future and see possibilities for a person. She did one on me to make sure I would come home. Things were not rosy for me, she told me, but I would survive and get home in one piece. She told me to pack. My wardrobe was, shall we say, conservative; it mostly consisted of jeans, T-shirts and trainers. I also got a collection of CDs for the journey. Flight time to Mars 2 was approximately three days. As it was my first time up, Reece offered to show me the sights of the solar system. I especially wanted to see

Jupiter and Saturn up close. Reece said that was not a problem; we would be undetected by Earth radar. Ripple radar had not been invented yet. I said my goodbyes to my mother, father and sister and told them I was going abroad with my friend but was not sure when I would be home but not to worry.

It was time to go. Beam us up, Mitchel!

The teleporter was a bit of an anti-climax. It was like a cupboard with no door. There was a small computer to one side where you entered your coordinates and a projection scanner to make sure you came back. Mitchel greeted us and said, 'I suppose you would like a look round?' 'You bet I do!' I said.

At the front of the ship, there was the cockpit for pilot and co-pilot with a big curved viewing screen from which I could see the Earth. It was very luxurious like a Ferrari crossed with an ultra-modern digital control system. The main computer was to the rear of the cockpit. It was a glass box with some cubes connected to a central hub. I had never seen a computer like this before. Mitchel explained the specifications. The memory was non-organic but could grow to increase memory capacity if needed. The main interface was an android that could walk around the ship and operate its systems. It had an IQ of 300 and could master new tasks very quickly. Its main job was co-piloting and also going into hazardous areas, for instance, high radiation or toxic gases where the crew could not go. As I was looking round, I saw 'him' sitting in the tower. This was the best seat in the house.

You could fly the ship solo from the tower, and the tower had the only forward-facing window on the ship.

As we walked down the narrow corridor to the back of the ship, we next passed the drop ship hangar. This was the only area of the ship that they were secretive about. The technology on the drop ship was the most advanced on the ship. It was capable of vertical take-off and landing and could reach escape velocity on planets with double the Earth's gravitational field. It was also radar invisible. I was dying for a go in it.

Next, there was an entertainment room with an entertainer system. It had a vast library of music and films and was a great place to relax.

We then went past the crew quarters. The ship was designed with a crew of four in mind and also room for a couple of passengers. There were half a dozen bedrooms with en suite, and they were all very comfortable.

Next up was the suspended animation room. This was used for long-haul flights in excess of three months. While the crew were in stasis, the computer would run the ship and revive us if need be.

Next was the bowels of the ship. The main reactor and drive systems. The reactor was powered by a quantum interface powering the ship's systems and drive system. The main drive was a multi-system drive configuration for sub-light and hyperdrive conditions. The ship also had artificial gravity. Instead of the whole floor being on all the time, the gravity system used local gravity. It would track you around the ship and the gravity system would follow you around. Mitchel demonstrated using a ball. Mitchel threw a ball very gently and it travelled linearly at a constant speed down the corridor without falling to the deck while we were firmly held to the floor. Most impressive.

Reece came to see how we were getting on and was pleased. She then started to explain some of the other aspects of the ship's functions. It was used to transport things, mostly tobacco and coffee. The ship was also armed with smart missiles and had a black hole generator for self-defence. This was made possible by having a local generator. It is a device that can change the local laws of physics. She would not say where she got that from.

The journey from the Sol system went smoothly. We did a flyby of Jupiter, then Saturn, which was spectacular, and then headed off into deep space. We engaged hyperdrive after Saturn and headed to Mars 2. The remarkable thing about the ship was that it was almost silent, and you could not feel the acceleration of the craft as we approached the speed of light. Pretty soon we were at cruising speed of 550 times the speed of light. I felt I was still connected to Earth by some kind of umbilical cord. When we were nearly a light year out, I felt it break and then I knew I had popped my cherry. I was now a proper deep space explorer.

Mitchel had jobs to do, so I got to sit in the cockpit with Reece and watch the stars fly by. Reece was quite mysterious. She told me she was a distant relative from my mother's side. I asked her about the ship, and she told me in fact it was stolen. She did not seem to care about consequences. She told me Discovery 2 was built on the moon in the 22nd century and that she and Mitchel stole it. She was hiding out in time.

I asked about Mitchel. Reece laughed. 'Mitchel', she said, 'was the president of the USA from the mid-21st century'. I was gobsmacked. But flying around in a starship was more fun than running a country, and he called it a perk of his job. Nobody aged on starships either. Discovery 2 had a fountain of youth.

We started to make our approach to Mars 2. Mars 2 were requesting our authorisation code for landing. I heard Reece saying that I was on board.

Mars 2 got its name for its similarity to our Mars in the Sol system. It also had ice reserves below the surface, making it ideal to set up a base. The base itself has a striking resemblance to Moon Base Alpha from *Space 1999*. No accident, I thought to myself. We landed softly and docked successfully. I stood by the door and waited for the airlock to pressurise. A red light came on, the door opened and we were free to enter. For some reason, Mars 2 uses red for go and green for stop.

We walked down a glass corridor to the main complex. There were models of various starships as decoration. I don't know how many were real or just made up, but they were fascinatingly imaginative. I got the feeling they were expecting us as we were ushered through security very quickly. There was a base map on the wall, and we followed it to the living quarters area. Reece and I had been assigned a twin room to share; Mitchell was staying with a friend. The room was very much like a Holiday Inn, but the view from the window was the giveaway. We unpacked our things, and then I asked Reece, 'Is there a pub?' Yes, there was, and that is where we headed next; I was also hungry. The pub was the most retro part of the base. It was stone construction with a well in the middle of the floor, which I was told led to hell. There was a strange red glow coming from it, so I didn't go too close. The bar had an excellent sound system and belted out some absolute classics, some I had not heard before. We had a good night and retired around midnight. We would be leaving tomorrow night.

In the morning, we grabbed breakfast from the canteen. Reece then took me to the command centre to meet the head scientist, Arthur Koenig. He was God when it came to science and was reputedly hundreds of years old. It is thought he came from Earth, but no one was sure. He used a theory called 'Third', which allowed for matter manipulation, which is how the base was constructed. The downside was that some of his failures had been on a gigantic scale, and he had a very chequered past. But apparently he was cheap and enjoyed his work.

We were ready to go. Then came the big question: do I want to return to Earth, or do I want to go with Reece and Mitchell? Had I any sense, I think I should have gone home. I had already seen some amazing things, but I thought this was a once-in-a-lifetime opportunity. Reece pointed out we would be away for around 20 years. Admittedly a lot of it in suspended animation. I missed out on Concorde once, so I thought, what the hell.

The first trips were milk runs round the Common. The Common is where Earth is along with about half a dozen other worlds. The technology levels are within about 400 years of each other, and it is classified as a good neighbourhood. I was also told about funnel web systems. They are star systems with advanced technology levels but do not explore space. If you enter their star systems, they will capture and kill you. It is as simple as that. Hence, good star maps cost a lot of money; they could save your life. Another area to avoid was the Aerial, one of the most advanced civilisations in our section of the galaxy. They were called the Aerial because after a war, all that remained was an aerial on a planet. This area is off limits as is the inner section of the galaxy.

Reece and Mitchell made their money by trading on a kind of interstellar stock market. Interplanetary trading is big business and can make you a lot of money. This is another reason why they were interested in me having heard my exploits as an apprentice at the ATA. I took to it like a duck to water. One of our biggest sellers was coffee. You could charge a fortune for it on deep-space colonies. We made a lot of money. We spent the next 15 years heading deeper and deeper into space finding new products to sell. By this time we were very rich.

We were now out 7,800 light years from Earth and were on our last stop before heading home. The planet of the Murgher (pronounced the 'murder'). They were one of the oldest races in the galaxy. They were hammerheads, like the sharks, quite scary to look at but very nice people. They were the best starship builders in our quadrant. And that is why we were there. I had all this money and hadn't spent a penny. A new ship for myself was in order.

The ships were of various specifications, from planet hoppers to true galaxy-class starships. You could also choose the level of technology you required. I opted for a ship similar to Discovery 2 but updated and superior. The ship was a beauty. In car terms, she was a Lamborghini, 50 metres long and as black as the ace of spades. She was mine. I decided to call her Discovery 3.

The most memorable part of this journey was our last dinner in a restaurant near the space port. It was just myself and Reece, and it was quite romantic. The restaurant prided itself on providing cuisine for all races from anywhere in the galaxy. I had the beef stroganoff. It was delicious.

So this was it. Reece, Mitchell and I were to part ways. I was going to head back to Mars 2; Reece and Mitchell had other business. I did hope to see them again. Discovery 2 was already in orbit, and they waited for me to rendezvous with them to return to our sector. The Murgher had built a hyperdrive super highway which we were going to use to get most of the way home. It used a carrier wave, allowing ships to break 700 times the speed of light. This was much quicker and would reduce journey time by a factor of four. We were really moving; the stars were stretched like a special effect from *Star Wars* or *Star Trek*. The ship was on autopilot, so I had time to read the owner's manual of my new ship.

Chapter 9

Discovery 3 was a beauty. She had a similar layout to Discovery 2 but was superior in many ways. There was a standard two-man cockpit in the nose and a tower where the ship could be flown solo. The ship operated by voice command and manual programming. Piloting the ship from the tower was like driving a bus, a very fast bus. She could to zero to 50% the speed of light in 10 seconds. The ship's star map was also second to none and had all funnel webs in our quadrant. There was enough information for centuries of exploring. The med lab was the pinnacle of Murgher technology. You could do practically anything with it from complex operations, cancer treatment and regeneration. The cancer treatment came in very handy, as I had leukaemia during my time on the ship. To keep me amused, there was a couple of tech labs to play with: one with android kits and another with a teleport kit.

The androids came in three varieties, types 1, 2 and 3. I considered type 1 to be the most beautiful. They were a bit like very high-tech meccano with a latex-type skin. They were also lighter than a comparative human. Type 2 were a more modular construction and slightly heavier. Then there was type 3. These were solid state, for want of a better description, and by far the most powerful both physically and mentally. They were best able to mimic a human and were very fast learners. Their IQ was similar to that of a ship's computer. Type 3's gave me the creeps, but thankfully they could be shut down several ways including voice command and remote control. They all had an on off button on their back. To keep myself amused, I built a type 1, but it spent most of its time in a cupboard.

Building the teleport was great fun. I opted for a style of teleportation portrayed on the television programme *Blake's 7*. I programmed the ship's computer to evaluate the best and fastest system. We came up with a thing I called the Terminator constant. This was the transfer speed from one location to the next. If you tried to transport faster than this, the system would fail. To operate it, I made a simple terminal with a scanner capable of finding suitable coordinates. It also incorporated a projection computer for safety reasons. I could communicate with it through a com bracelet although I programmed it to use telepathy for emergencies. Being the only one in the ship, I decided not to use the teleport unless I really had to.

My first stop in Discovery 3 was Mars 2. I went there to file a flight plan and to pick up some music for my voyage. The life of the ship was 100 Earth years, so I set a plan accordingly. I opted to do some exploration. This is not a common thing; in space, most journeys are for trade or political reasons. I decided to plot my course in an area where there was no intelligent life and away from the funnel webs. I came across a number of Earth-like worlds. The more I found, the more interesting our Earth appeared.

Nearly all the habitable planets I came across had 90% water and 10% land mass. Also, there were no large animals, either mammals or lizards. But there were birds. None of them had a moon like our own. It made me realise how special Earth really is.

I decided to stake claim on these planets, which would require landing. This would mean using the drop ship. This was going to be tricky, as I had never flown a drop ship before; I could barely fly an aeroplane. That is when I discovered the hat box. The hat box had hats that would give you the knowledge to do things you had no experience of, for instance, maintaining a quantum reactor. You simply put the hat for the job and then, using telepathy, you would have expert skills. Being on my own, help from the ship's sentinel or the android I built came in handy.

So I got my hat, jumped in the cockpit and away I went. It was a weird sensation. On the one hand I was confident, and on the other I was terrified. It was then that I felt like a real astronaut for the first time. The buffeting of re-entry and the glow from the nose were familiar from television but exhilarating. I turned on the ground-scanning radar and found somewhere good to land. The ship had vertical take-off and landing, so this was not too difficult. The atmosphere checked out, and so I did not need my pressure suit.

I climbed out of the cockpit through the belly hatch. I had bought with me some apple saplings. I got the idea from Jonny Appleseed. I thought it may make an interesting discovery for someone who visited the planet from Earth after me. A conundrum: It felt lonely on this planet and was the most alone I had ever felt. I decided not to hang around and returned to Discovery 3.

I realised loneliness was going to be a problem, so I had to do something about this. I could return to Earth and get a crew together, but who could I trust? Discovery 3 was the most desirable ship in our sector. Some would kill to get on the ship. I thought about heading back to Mars 2, but it had a high riff-raff factor, so that was out. My solution: make a companion! I had the technology, the time and the expertise to do this. I also decided to make the ship's computer more human as well. Instead of a sentinel, I changed her into a Marilyn Monroe lookalike, much nicer than the robotic-looking doorman. The functionality was still the same, but it was much easier on the eye.

When I bought the ship, the Murgher had imprinted my DNA and brain signature to it. They also took the liberty of making me a 'spare' should I have a fatal accident. The equipment could do just about anything you could think of. Full brain transplants and repair to the body from what would ordinarily be fatal injuries. Tied in with the teleport and projection computer, I essentially had unlimited lives while on the ship or within range of her.

So to build a companion, I opted for female, five foot three and blonde. She was attractive but not my cup of tea, as I would be in essence her father. The IQ I made about the same as mine, around the 130 mark. I also made her of slight build should something go wrong and I needed to restrain her. She would be 21 years old at creation. Young enough to ask questions, old enough to have a moral compass. Although she was a readymade human, she needed nursing for the first few months and teaching to eat and attend to personal hygiene. Once she was competent with this, I switched her over to ship protocol.

You did not need to go to the toilet or eat on Discovery 3. The transporter could do that for you. It could evacuate your bowels and could feed you directly into your stomach. Very convenient. To evacuate your bowels, you pressed your lower abdomen and to eat rubbed your tummy. It was a very neat arrangement. But it did make you appreciate good food. The replicator on board could facilitate this. I saved proper meals for Sundays.

I decided to name my new companion Anne. 'Anne Discovery Three'. The training went very quickly and well, and soon we were good crewmates. Anne loved the ship's library; it had books on anything you could think of and some stuff you would never have thought of. During my time with Anne, I became a very skilled physician and made Earth's conventional medication (21st century) look literally like the Spanish Inquisition. The plan was to bring these skills back home on my return.

Now I had Anne with me, sightseeing was the order of the day. I took her all over the quadrant. One of the stupidest things we did was to go and see the Aerial. We were sure we could outrun them if they caught us; Discovery 3 was very fast, fast enough to outrun a cube. So we went for a look. We travelled through several dead systems until our scanners found the Aerial point of origin, so we went in closer. The first cube appeared. We needed to get the hell out of there. They were predators, they were a funnel web and we should have known better. We hit maximum acceleration to get out of Aerial space. They were hot on our heels. I got the computer to try and squeeze as much speed as it could from the hyperdrive system. We got away by the skin of our teeth.

To be honest, we had become complacent and a bit cocky. Discovery 3 was an awesome ship but even she had limitations. We went back to the original plan of finding unpopulated life-bearing planets. In total we found 50. I planted apple trees on them all. After our brush with the Aerial, we called the section of space 'Damnation Alley'.

There were two other memorable planets. One was nicknamed Ziest, and the other was an android planet. Zeist had been unoccupied for a few centuries; apparently there was a biological war that wiped out the entire population: a fate that may await man. The technology was similar to that of 21st-century Earth as was the architecture. I found the planet fascinating and could not wait to go down for a closer look. The dead occupants were humanoid judging by the skeletons. I decided to have a look round one of the cities and landed on the outskirts. I had scrambler bikes on board, and these were ideal for exploration. Anne was holding the ship. It seemed incredible that a race could be left to this fate. Why had nobody intervened? Maybe there was some truth in the Star Trek Prime Directive regarding 'local systems'. That is up to 700 light years away. After about half an hour, I had seen enough and left a wreath out of respect before returning to the ship.

The android planet was remarkable. A whole planet of androids with its own laws and ways. This was a common stop off for space travellers. Their hospitality was second to none, and they loved to meet new races to add to their data. The ones we met were of human appearance. I think they changed the way they looked depending on the guests. They took local currency and offered five-star luxury. This was the first chance we had to actually spend some money. I was still very rich, in fact richer. The company was doing very well. This was a good place to go for information. We found out that Anne and I were becoming famous. We were called the 'Only', and our exploits were well documented. In most cases, no one had ever seen a human or even heard of us. We were a good 300 years ahead of our time. Even the occupants of Mars 2 did not venture very far.

At 40 years out, we were in the neighbourhood of Earth, and I decided to make a quick stop off. Anne was dead set against it and said we should go by, but I was sure nothing would go wrong. Anne asked to be dropped off at Mars 2 while I went home for a social call. She had full access to accounts and would be comfortable until my return. The year was around 2050.

Once I was within one light year of Earth, I started to pick up BBC2. I did a flyby of Saturn and decided to take a look at Titan with the drop ship. Even though I had travelled to many star systems, Titan was particularly interesting. I dove down into the thick atmosphere and saw the fantastic landscape. There were mountains and valleys; some of the mountains would dwarf Everest. It was a thrilling ride.

It was a long time since I had been home, and a lot had changed. Most of my family were dead and most of my friends. I was not in 2050 for long. The ship had orders from the Murgher. The original programme was for a 100-year voyage. The ship would get me home and then deactivate. They did not tell me not to return to Earth until the 100 years was up. I got a brief look at 2050, then the ship took me back in time to 1990 a few days after I left with Reece. That is when the problems started. The ship was programmed with a hindsight clause. The future me could countermand past-me orders. This works fine if you are compos mentis. Unfortunately, future me was not, which I did not know at the time. There was an incident from 1991 where I was tortured. The mad me attacked my future self from 1996. I had some crazy idea that I would steer through history using pain and time loops until I took the correct path. This was hell; there was no other way to describe it. Death was preferable to this. The ship had been one step ahead of this and reduced pain levels by stretching time, so it felt like being in a hot bath. Mad me thought it was too slow and decided to try and compress time to get it over and done with more quickly. This made the pain levels terrifying. The ship using the future orders tried to calculate maximum pain for shortest duration. Essentially it was calculating hell. I tried to shut the computer down, but it would not follow my orders. There was a form of control-alt-delete the ship's computer used, saying 'no' three times. This did not work. The computer then made itself live so I would get a shock if I tried to stop it. The only chance I had left was the gun that was designed to destroy the CPU. Through excruciating pain,

I managed to fire the gun and shut down the computer for good. Discovery 3 was now dead. There was no way I could get a new computer on Earth. I put Discovery 3 up for sale; she was no good to me now. The money would go through to my Mars 2 account.

***

The only thing left to do now was go home. I went to the teleport, checked the projection and found suitable coordinates to beam down. It was outside Barclays bank on Lord Street, two minutes' walk from where I lived. I still had my keys and let myself in and went straight to my room. I turned on the light, TV and the radio. 'Ordinary World' by Duran Duran was playing. This song was not released until 1994. This was the first time I had heard music ahead of time on Earth.

My father knocked on my door to see how I was. He saw I was a bit upset and asked what was wrong. Nothing, I told him. Who would believe me if I told them my story? A weird thing that happened to me while I was away was I forgot what idioms meant. For instance, one I found particularly confusing was 'to put your foot down'. Why would I want to put my foot down? What is special about my foot? While I was away, I stopped using such idioms.

I was now around 80 years old and had regenerated twice. Living without the ship was going to be difficult. Having to use a toilet again and eating every day would take some adjustment. I did find it surprisingly easy to get back into my life and reconnect with people. To them I went away for a few days. Something I did find hard was not being a billionaire. I was just an airframe fitter with a habit of spending money like it was water.

I decided to get straight back to work. Cambridge Aerotech offered me work in Frankfurt again with Billy, which I snapped up. It was fun going to Germany to work for 48 hours, then go home, then back again. The Gulf War show was still on at the airport. As a general, I would go to Iraq.

***

I got my marching orders from General Schwarzkopf. I was to meet at the American airbase and would be flown to the war zone. I was given a VIP ride to the Gulf. While the troops were on troop carrier aircraft, I got to fly on an F14 Tomcat. We flew over France, something I always enjoy; they have a beautiful country. After in-flight refuelling, I requested supersonic clearance. It was given. It was a bit like being on a primitive drop ship. The ground was whizzing by. My role in the gulf was CO of Delta Force. There wasn't much to do; it was a token post. They already had their orders and knew what was expected of them. My real mission there was something very different. We were worried the Iraqis would destroy some of the historical artefacts. My job was bell-mine raiding. I met up with an AV8B pilot who was going to take me to the bell mines. It was the scrolls we were after. They contained prophecies. We landed close by the bell mine, and I got out and abseiled into the mine. We were after particular ones, and I was given a book with drawings to match with the scrolls. We collected about a dozen scrolls and took them back to HQ for analysis.

While at HQ, I ran into Colonel Rimington. It was good to see her. I asked her what MI5 were doing in Iraq. She told me they were field-testing phasers. She said they were not very good and needed a lot more development. They were also riding shotgun in Tornados on bombing missions; the job was to look out for enemy fighters and warn the pilot. Sounded like great fun.

Schwarzkopf heard I was about and came to say hello. He asked me if I wanted to take a stealth bomber up; it could take off, navigate and land all on autopilot if need be. Ground crew would prep the aircraft for me. I got in and felt right at home; it reminded me of the drop ship on Discovery 3 and should be no problem to handle even with the autopilot off. So I taxied down the runway and got clearance to take off. It would just be a quick circuit and then land again. Take-off was smooth and controlled. I got up a few thousand feet and then began to turn. The rudder appeared to be jammed. I don't know if I was hit or whether it was a mechanical fault. I lost control of the aircraft and banged out. The plane went down in a fireball, and I landed about a mile away from the wreck. Ejecting from an aircraft is not nice. The initial blast of the rocket motor usually puts you out. The force also compresses your spine. When I landed, I felt like I had been beaten up by a gorilla. An ambulance appeared after a few minutes and took me to the field hospital. I was OK, only minor bumps and bruises. They then sent me home.

***

Over the few weeks before Christmas, I picked up a couple of shifts at Frankfurt airport with Billy. I enjoyed telling him my tales of derring-do while in Iraq. I was not that concerned about money at the time because I knew I would be paid for *Terminator 2*. It was due for release in August 1991. The film had advanced screening for the troops. It was the in-flight movie for the journey to Iraq. From the feedback from the troops, it was clear that it was going to be a massive hit.

Christmas that year was a bit of a blur of alcohol and cannabis. I spent it partying hard. This was the last Christmas at Raffles. Gary was selling up; I was really sad to see him go. It was the best rock club I ever went to, there was never any trouble and the music was the best rock in town. I heard that he was selling up to some Hells Angels. I knew it would not be the same.

Just before Christmas, I got my first big break with Cambridge Aerotech. We had a German Cargo contract to do a major service on a DC8 cargo plane. The plan was to turn it round in six weeks maximum. And I was selected. The contract began in January. There were about 80 of us in all. We were doing 12-hour shifts day and night. The money was good too. It was the best I had ever been offered: £14.60 per hour, about £1,000 per week. The bosses decided that to make it fair, we would alternate between night and day shifts. Nobody was happy with this; we all said the same thing. We wanted to work all days or all nights for the duration of the contract. They said no. This meant you got a 24-hour weekend before having to switch to days from nights and vice versa. This really took its toll on me. It was very exhausting work. Physically I was a wreck. The injection for Iraq was giving me chronic fatigue, and my mental health was also deteriorating. Some of the other guys noticed this. Some were supportive, and some took advantage of me. A couple of the older guys took me under their wing. It kept the wolves away.

We finished the aircraft in five weeks, one week ahead of schedule. We had won the maintenance contract for German Cargo DC8s. The next plane was due in for a major service in two weeks. There was a team photo taken that was published in *Flight* magazine. Billy and I were hiding by the coffee machine when the picture was taken.

I was glad to be out of there. As I had money in my pocket, I decided to take the scenic route home. I caught a train, with a couple of the others, to Paris and then flew back to Manchester from Charles De Gaul. A couple of others came with me. I did not think I could handle another one of these contracts. It was simply too much for my body and mind. I was due to get paid by James Cameron in April, so I decided to sit out the next contract with Cambridge Aerotech.

I spent a lot of time in my room listening to music and watching television. I also smoked a lot of cannabis, which was having a negative impact on my failing mental health.

In March 1991 I had visitors. Lady Jane turned up with her cronies, and three members of Def Leppard came to meet me. Sadly I did not have much in common with the Leppards. They all liked football and Subbuteo, which I thought was crap. The lead singer was a bit of an egotist, but I liked Rick the drummer and Phil the guitarist. They were nice to me.

On 12 March 1991, my problems really started. Lady Jane wanted me to pledge my allegiance to her. I told her that I was loyal to the Queen. It did not go down well at all. Lady Jane was furious with me. She was going to get her own back but would leave it for months or even years. Her plans were very cruel. Some said I was cowardly; others said I was a very brave man for standing up to her like that. I found myself with new enemies but also new allies.

Lady Jane and her entourage left, and life returned to sort of normal. I decided to try a new contracting agency. They were called A-Tech, based at Heathrow Airport. They asked me to attend an interview in Bolton of all places, at my father's old hotel! We were to meet in the communal area. I was overflowing with confidence and wore jeans, a T-shirt and trainers. I showed him my diploma from the ATA, and then he asked me the interview questions. I found them easy. He had one really difficult question up his sleeve which he saved for last. It was a technical question about a certain aircraft I had never worked on. He told me in the scenario that none of the team knew the answer. I said I would ring the manufacturer customer support for technical advice. I was the only person he ever interviewed who came up with an answer to that question. We shook hands; he said they will be in touch in a couple of weeks. I left confident that I got the job.

When I got home, I told my father, who was very pleased for me. The days went by, and there was no word; I was still confident, but my father was not so sure. But then, when he was about to give up on me, I got the call. I started the following Saturday and was to go to Heathrow Airport for my joining instructions. I had a bit of money, so I decided to fly there from Liverpool.

A-Tech came across as a slick operation. Most of the staff were ex-services, so I was a bit of an odd one out there. I was most notable because of my Mick Jagger haircut. After signing some paperwork, I was introduced to Andy, the team senior. Andy had been with A-Tech for many years and would show me the ropes. We went over the road from the office to the hotel where we would be sharing a room. I got on with Andy straightaway. He was ex–air force and about 20 years older and wiser than me. We had some food and couple of pints and then went to bed early. We were on the first flight to Munich in the morning.

Morning came and I was quite excited. I knew nothing of Munich and imagined it would be a bit like Frankfurt. We boarded our flight with Lufthansa and found ourselves at the back of the aircraft with the cabin crew, which was getting to be normal for aircraft contracting. The flight was quick and without incident. The contract manager, Colin, was there to meet us at arrivals.

The hotel was about a half-hour drive from the airport. Munich countryside is beautiful, and the village/town where the hotel was was very picturesque. The hotel was at the top of a hill. There were probably about 20 of us in all. We were split between two hotels because of politics. At the time, there was a war going on in old Yugoslavia between Croats and Serbs. Half of us were at a Serb-run hotel, and the other half were at a Croat hotel.

Being the new boy, I got the shitty end of the stick. My room was in the basement of the hotel. Everyone else in our hotel had their own en suite room. It was still better than the other hotel where the guys were in dorms. Once I had unpacked and freshened up, I headed to the bar/restaurant to meet the others. They were all very friendly. About five of us were airframe fitters, and the other half were aircraft sprayers. They were on about £2.50 an hour less than us but still a lot of money for a sprayer. The guys were also fiercely patriotic, which I was very pleased about. With our first round of drinks, we drank a toast to the Queen.

The food at the pension was excellent. It was a bit German and a bit Serbian. There was a lot of pork. The chef was excellent and varied the menu every week for us, as we would be there for three months. The company provided us with two VW Polos to get to work and get around. We could use them for social purposes and also to go to the laundrette. Some of the guys treated the cars like shit. 'If it breaks we just get a new one' was their mentality. I took a dim view.

Monday morning was my first day at Dornier Aerospace in Oberpaffenhoffan. It took about 20 minutes from the pension. There was a big carpark outside the gate; we parked up and went to security to get our passes. The setup was a bit like RAF St Athan, military and well-guarded. They took our pictures, and we had our IDs in about an hour. Once that was done, I went to the hangar I would be working in. My aircraft was a Dornier 228. I had never seen one before. They were used for Arctic survey work. There were two in the hangar. At the far end, there were four private jets. The man I was working with was ex-RAF and took an instant dislike to me; I think it was my hair. He spoke German at every opportunity and tried to cut me out of everything. Luckily he was in a very small minority; I got on well with the others.

The job was very easy; they were simple repairs and no impending deadline. The private jets were particularly interesting. I had only ever seen them on TV. The first opportunity I got, I went for a look inside. Most of them were six-seaters. Cessna Citations and Canadair Challengers, which were slightly bigger. The seats were plush leather and very comfortable. You could see why these planes cost millions. One of them had a cockpit more advanced than a Tornado!

Chapter 10

In Munich, I ran into Rachael again although I think it was not by accident. It was at an Inspiral Carpets gig in the city; they were playing with EMF. She told me there was someone she would like me to meet. His name was Vince. Between sets, Rachael introduced us. Vince was road crew for the Carpets. On first impressions, I thought he looked a bit like Parker, the chauffer in *Thunderbirds*. He told me he was starting a new band with his brother and that they would be mega famous. Couldn't knock him for enthusiasm! He was looking for writers to collaborate with, and he wanted to work with me, having heard of my success with Def Leppard. He told me they would be in touch.

The night life in Munich was both dismal and very expensive. The best bar we found was an Irish bar in the centre of the city. The music was OK, but they did play a lot of Gilbert O'Sullivan, which reminded me of my worst days of childhood and made me depressed. Fortunately, everyone spoke English, and the beer was not too extortionate. A couple of weeks later, I heard Lady Jane was having a private party at the Irish bar, and I was invited along with a couple of guests of my choosing. None of the lads were particularly keen surprisingly. One of the sprayers wanted to go, so I brought him along. I had never been to anything like it before. There were TV cameras and lights everywhere. And I knew a few of the guests from boarding school. Murph was there with his cronies, and Miller was there, who I spent most of the night talking to. In hindsight, talking to Miller was like having a chat with the devil. He was very well connected and respected. A smooth operator. He knew about my run-in with Lady Jane and said I was very gutsy. The conversation got around to movies. He knew about *Terminator 2*. He wanted me to make up a story plot off the top of my head. I was not so sure and tried to emphasise that these stories took weeks or even months to put together. He was undeterred. The film was *Last Action Hero*. I washed my hands of it and warned them it would be a flop. They did not listen. The conversation then got around to aircraft, and the Ganzenhoef scenario reared its ugly head again. Miller tried to talk me through the emergency landing procedure. I felt like we were putting our heads in a fire. I had a bad feeling about this plane, and so did some of the others listening in. I decided talking to Miller was only going to get worse, so I took a beeline for Murph.

We had not seen each other in years, and it was great to see him again. He was with a friend who I nicknamed 'Golden Gob', as all of his molars were gold. He wore an ill-fitting Saville Row suit and chain-smoked, dropping ash down his front. He could have been a James Bond villain. He didn't say very much; we talked about what we were doing these days. Murph and Golden Gob were both on allowances from their wealthy parents and spent their time looking for the next 'big thing'. Mary came up in the conversation, and like the devil, she appeared. She came over to say hello and put her hand on mine; she seemed pleased to see me. Stephen Fry, who happened to be there, overheard me saying that she was stonking. He had never heard the expression before. 'Let's stonk!' said Stephen Fry to everyone in the bar.

Lady Jane had made a block booking at a local hotel, so I did not have to go back to my pension. I think someone put something in my drink; when I got to my room, I was very weak and by my standards had drunk very little. I remember lying naked on the bed when a woman came in topless and wearing bikini bottoms. She sat across me and began tapping my left testicle with her fingernail. At first, it was just mildly annoying, but it then became a dull, heavy pain. I tried to get her off, but I was too weak. I don't know how long this went on for, but I passed out. I remember having an out-of-body experience. I was stood above the bed watching her. After I stopped responding, she threw me around the room. I hit my head against a cabinet and broke one of my upper front teeth. She left me for dead.

The next thing I remember was Lady Jane above me shaking me and saying, 'Live, you son of a bitch!' I came round. A doctor came and gave me a once-over. I would live. I got in the shower to freshen up then went to bed. Then there was a knock on the door. I looked through the security eyehole, and it was Mary. I let her in. She heard what had happened and came to comfort me. *Fair consolation*, I thought. It made the worst night of my life almost bearable. I woke the next morning to find I was in bed with a strange man! Mary must have done a switch. It fitted her sense of humour. I was a little horrified and amused as well. I got dressed and decided to go back to the bar to see if any of the staff noticed anything fishy last night. Nobody saw a thing. I had a beer and then Murph arrived. He asked if I was hungry, and we went to a restaurant with a few others for something to eat. I told Murph what happened. He said that I was Micky Finned. I still felt awful, and to make it worse, I was whistling when I spoke because of my broken front tooth.

The next day, I was back in the hotel room in Munich with Murph. He was doing a surveillance operation, watching a hotel across the way with a telescope. Lady Jane popped by to see how it was going. She saw my tooth and said she will get a dentist to sort it out. After about 20 minutes, the dentist appeared and installed an implant for me. It was an excellent job and matched my old tooth perfectly. Later that day, things got a bit scary.

Murph was mixed up in something, I don't know what. I found out that Golden Gob was a 'driver'. They got me in their car and took me to their lair. Golden Gob was driving like a maniac, weaving in and out of the traffic and totally reckless and dangerous. I was used to scary driving during from my time in Wales, so I acted unperturbed. I think they were intending to kidnap me and to get Lady Jane to pay the ransom. After talking to me about Lady Jane, they realised that she would never pay and would enjoy my rough treatment. Stockholm syndrome. They showed me round. I had free reign of the camp. They had these things. I never figured out what they were. Rectangular metal blocks with handles. They told me they were transporter platforms for the SAS. They even left a military-issue pistol lying around, but I didn't touch it. Next day, they dropped me off at the pension, and I went back to work like nothing had happened.

Work passed quickly, and soon I was home again, big payday was not far off. From the response of the troops, we knew *Terminator 2* was a hit. The cheque came. It was a blank cheque! Being a smart aleck, I asked for £666,000. Anyone with half a brain would have requested at least a million! But I felt it was a fair price. House hunting began. I decided that living between South Wales and Southport would be the best idea. I found a place in Hereford called Dunbar; it was owned by Samantha Fox, the model. I snapped it up and paid cash for it, around £240,000. Lady Jane was still showing interest in me and asked me if her friend could move in with me as a lodger. Trying to curry favour, I agreed. Her name was Julia; she was a schoolteacher.

***

At my new home, to add to my catalogue of bad decisions, I decided to try worshiping Satan to see what would happen. Speak of the devil and he shall appear. He offered me various things, none of which caught my fancy. It was then he got cheesed off with me. He cursed me with songwriting that I would never make a penny from but would be very successful. Nothing new there then! He told me I would have to navigate past Lady Jane, as she was going to try and kill me. He told me the only way to manipulate time was to use pain. He then created a tau axis chamber for me to build a torture device in. A tau axis chamber is a chamber in space-time parallel to our reality but defies Pauli's exclusion principle. I had heard of these at the ATA. They sometimes open up on Tornado nose legs.

The torture device was a table that gave you the sensation of being bathed in boiling oil. This is where I became a second version of myself. There was now Evil Dave and frightened Dave, who would do no harm. As Evil Dave, I felt like I was a hijacked vehicle. I was possessed. I was there but not fully in control of my actions. Malfunctioning Discovery 3 was also in the mix; that is where the teleport was. This teleport could cross time. I did not know the ship could do this. Evil Dave beamed me in from 1996. He was angry because I had no money, no job and no friends. Frightened me did not know what to say other than 'Emergency teleport!' It worked the first time. But Evil Dave did not give up easily. He got me again, but this time I could not beam out. I was trapped. To my surprise, my friend Deb from Wales entered the room with a video camera to film everything. She had come down to Hereford for a visit. If something is on film, it is impossible to change using time travel. The reasons for this are quite complex. I was well and truly trapped. I think Deb thought she was trying to help. Video killed the radio star!

I was in the prone position lying on the table. It started off like a warm bath that gradually got hotter. I could feel it all over my body except my eyes. The pain was excruciating. The pain level went up and up. Level 1 like boiling water, level 2 like boiling oil, level 3 hell itself. I don't know how long I was on the thing for, but I think it was around 20 minutes. Finally it started to shut down. Reece and Discovery 2 had a hand in this. When it stopped, I got a shot in. Evil Dave was on the table now. I left him there and managed to beam out.

As Evil Dave I was trapped on the table for hours, many hours. Luckily for him/me, the setting was on level 1 by pure fluke. After a day or two, some soldiers came through and released me. They then smashed the machine up, thank God. I wished that nobody else would never have to endure this, even someone as reprehensible as Hitler!

Looking back, I am sure that I was possessed. Nobody would build a machine to torture themselves; it is not logical. My prime suspect was the gelatinous blob from my childhood that told me that he was the devil or Jabba the Hutt. There were many other instances of me getting tortured at Castle Close, but they were eclipsed by this event. I remember what happened, but when I became frightened, I wouldn't hurt a fly. Again, I felt like a force or presence had left my body, and I felt disjointed with the Evil Dave persona. The reality of what lay ahead for me was terrifying. My only consolation is I knew that I escaped.

To take my mind off it, I went back to work. I picked up a contract with Cambridge Aerotech working with Billy again. When I got home, Julia had changed all the locks, and I could not get in. She told me if I didn't go away that she would call the police. I told her to try it. She did and the police believed her, not me. So I had no choice but to go back to Southport.

When I got home, things had changed. My room was gone. All my stuff were in the bottom bedroom at the top of the stairs by the toilets. It was small but OK. My father called me the guard dog. Finding work was proving difficult. There was nothing with A-Tech or Cambridge Aerotech. I was left with no choice; I must get a job locally until something comes up. There was a press brake operator job going, operating CNC punching machines. The pay was abysmal, but it would keep the wolves from the door. The average IQ of the employees was very low. The job could have been done by a chimp. Within a week, I had the machines sussed and could write code for them. They moved me around various sections, and I picked up new skills. It did become apparent that the chargehand and floor supervisor did not like me, and I knew that my days were numbered. They were trying to get me to make a mistake so they could legitimately get rid of me. They eventually put me on the dodgiest machine they had. Nobody was supposed to use it. Even then, I managed to compensate for the flaws, so they got the inspector to lie so I would run off a bad batch. That was it, game over. They let me go about two weeks before Christmas. I was broke.

My father had no sympathy for me. I had no money for going out New Year's Eve to the Academy. He grudgingly gave me a fiver. The Academy had become the place to go after Gary sold Raffles. The new owner of Raffles scared away all the regulars with his Hells Angels friends. Mike H took over managing the Academy. He gave me a break and asked me if I would like to be the backup DJ so he could attend to other tasks. He offered me a tenner a night, but it kept the job centre off my back. So I said yes, and I really enjoyed it.

New year 1992, I managed to get another contract with A-Tech back at Dornier. Things were starting to look up. It wasn't megabucks, but it was enough especially if the contracts would be renewed. So off I went to Munich from Manchester. I got the train to the airport and picked up my ticket at the Lufthansa desk.

It was good to be back. I had missed the after-dinner chats we used to have and also the nickname they gave me, 'Zanusi', the appliance of science. Andy was there again as team leader, and I was put on the 228s again. Emotionally I was in a very dark place especially with the house thing, and I started to drink more heavily. The per diem was not enough because of my drinking; I was still drinking black Russians, which cost a bomb in Munich. I would have a drink with the guys' and then stay late at a crappy nightclub before getting a taxi back to the pension.

It was in a taxi one night that I was picked up by a female driver. We got chatting and found we had a lot in common. When she dropped me off, she gave me her number. So we had a little fling, which was a good distraction.

On the last weekend before we went home, we went to a beer festival down the road from where the pension was. A lady came over to talk to me. She said her name was Lady Luck. She told me never to return to Munich. She walked away and then returned. She told me I did return. Stupidly, I told her it was her fault, and I returned because she did not do her job properly. She became very angry with me, understandably. Andy told me to shut up, which I did, but it was too late. Lady Luck never smiled again until 13 December 1996.

I returned to my poky little room in my father's place. I spent most of my nights in the Academy DJing. Work seemed a really bad idea. There was no ban on Cambridge Aerotech, but I called and nothing was available. This went on for weeks. My father was unhappy with me; he called me a bum. There was only one solution: I needed to move out.

My mental health at this time was very poor, but I thought it was just me. I did not want to tell anyone because I thought they would call me weak and tell me to pull myself together. So I soldiered on. Then one day I had what could only be described as an episode. I had a mental excursion, and I was back in Iraq. I imagined the Saddam Hussein had blown up his own top-secret weapons facility by accident. It was like a Laurel and Hardy sketch. I was in the kitchen at the time, and I started laughing, but I could not stop. I tried lying on the work surface to try and contain myself, but I could not. This went on for about 20 minutes. Oddly enough, it was the same duration as my time in Evil Dave's torture chamber. The two were connected somehow.

In keeping with making bad decisions, I went to look at one flat and took it without looking at anything else. It was small but bigger than my box room at my father's. This was 13 Castle Close. The reason why I picked this flat was because it was used for a Hammer Horror movie in the early '70s. I thought a bit of notoriety would be a good talking point.

I moved in on 17 April 1992. The thing that sold it to me was the fact that there was a communal phone in the hall next to my flat so I could use it to get work. There was also a phone point in the flat, so I could get my own telephone.

The evening I moved in was strange and disturbing. Street lights were going out as I walked under them, and I felt like a presence was following me. I don't know if it was just me or something more sinister. If someone was controlling the lights, it would have been very expensive. My other thoughts were that it was Lady Jane doing it, but I have no idea how.

After a couple of weeks, the phone in the hall and phone point in my bedroom had been mysteriously removed. The carpet in the room was Ministry of Defence standard. I had had my wings clipped. I asked my father if he could take calls for me, but he wouldn't.

Then something happened that made the bad seem even worse. On 4 October 1992, El Al 747 cargo plane crashed in the Bijlmer neighbourhood in Amsterdam.

It was my worst nightmare. It was a Monday, and I went to get the paper across the road from the Academy. The front page was horrifying. Over 40 people had been killed, most on the ground. It felt like someone had insulted me on a very profound level. It gripped my heart with pain. I knew then that I should never return to aircraft maintenance. We did everything we could but still could not stop it. I felt like a used cigarette that has just been discarded, trodden on and crushed under foot. My head was getting more and more messed up. I had no one to talk to and no one to care. I sold my tools so I would not go back.

I started to hang round with another Deb who used to go to the Academy. She did not know what my career was and just assumed I as just another doley like her. We spent our time listening to music, playing games and smoking cannabis. It was my only escape from my troubles.

***

The flat was strange in a peculiar way. It always felt like I was being watched. I did a thorough search for fibre optic cameras and microphones but could not find anything. As time went by, this feeling became stronger and stronger. I began to hate the place but had no money with which to get out. The landlord, Geoffrey, became nastier and nastier. He knew I was ill and played on it.

The flat had a few maintenance issues which Geoffrey assured me he would sort out but never did. The tap washers on all the taps were perished, and the taps made a sort of hissing noise when turned off. After a while, I started to hear people talking out of the taps. I could not make it stop. I was scared to use to electric fire, as in the first instance those interface eye things came out of it which Colonel Rimington got rid of for me.

For a brief time, I had a TV but it broke. I could not afford to fix it. I still had my Sharp stereo though, and I could listen to music. I knew I was going to have a bad time at Castle Close, but I had a good collection of cassettes I had made in

Wales with over 100 albums to ease the torment. Frank and Ritchie turned up and Frank took all my tapes, saying they were his. Richie was his sidekick that day, so things got worse.

One night, I saw a phantom in the flat. It was the head of a cowboy holding a gun, and it went round the room. I thought it was a projection, but there was no source.

***

Before the malfunction of Discovery 3 we set up an underground base directly under Castle Close. I called it 'Down Stairs'. It was accessed by teleport. There was the main ship bay; starships could use the industrial teleport to land in the bay. Reece had a house down there at the far end of the bay, but she would never let me in. I had a trading lounge where I could administer my business and a bedroom. I also had a Cyclops 5 defence computer, which proved to be expensive and useless, and a medical bay, which, while not as good as the one on Discovery 3, was still years ahead of Earth circa 1992. There was also an experimental fusion reactor in the bay I had been working on.

The interfaces started to get into the base. I think Koenig had been there, as the technology involved was right up his street. There was a star freighter in there, which is where I thought they came from. The interfaces had a long term effect on me. Once you got one on your eyes, they were almost impossible to remove. The view from them was simply a white room with white walls, ceiling and floors. It literally bored you to death! One saving grace was that they could not reach the surface. The teleport could get rid of them when returning to the surface. I think they were put there to stop me going down there. Nobody else was affected, that is, Reece and Mitchell. Their place was bomb-proof and had its own teleport. I decided to destroy the base. I could not take any more of the interfaces. Time downstairs went as with the surface, but the teleport always put you back microseconds after beaming down. So I could spend a year Down Stairs and only be gone for a microsecond. Also, with this setup you did not physically age. By this time, including the time in space, I must have been well over 100 years old.

From 1992 to 1994, I tried to spend as much time as I could away from Castle Close. IT was making life hell for me. IT made me throw food in the bin when I had little enough to eat. The grip of IT went 100 yards in all directions from the flat. The local library was my sanctuary. I spent all week days there from opening to closing.

I visited Mike S and Deb as much as I could and also spent a lot of time at the Academy. Mike S was always sympathetic to my condition. He knew I was ill but I didn't. Deb probably just thought I was a bit strange. We played computer games at Mike's on his Amiga and talked about science fiction and new aircraft. They also used to feed me, which was very nice of them. I used to make the tea. At Debs, we would listen to music and smoke cannabis. We also used to write songs, but they were not very good.

My love life at the time was not very good. I hadn't seen Sally for a couple of years, and there was no one in Southport who fitted the bill. I think that the girls from Wales were nicer-looking. But my luck did change. I met a girl called Mandy at the Academy. At the time, she had a young daughter and lived in a much nicer flat than me. We dated for about five weeks, and I spent as much time as I could there to the point that she used to send me home for a break. Her cooking was good, and she reminded me of Delia Smith. Mandy knew I was ill too, and it became too much for her, so she broke up with me.

My wardrobe was falling apart, and I had no money to replace my clothes and shoes. I also had the problem of an evil presence, IT, which made me throw my money away literally. I think I picked up a curse when I was raiding the bell mines. I also think that Lady Jane hexed me. I was in quite a state. The noise from the taps was getting worse, and I kept on trying to stop it by talking to the computer from Discovery 3. Obviously futile. Then the time loops started. These were horrible to the point that I wanted to commit suicide. I kept reliving bad days over and over again. It was soul destroying, and I could not make it stop.

Things drudged along for the next couple of years, and I became desperate. I got in touch with A-Tech and asked if there were any contracts going in Munich. I used the phone box at the end of the road. I got a job despite having no tools. I was so glad to be away from there I thought, *Damn the consequences. How bad could it be?*

I had enough money for the train to get to Manchester Airport and was travelling very light. It was January 1995 and still very wintery in Munich. The village we stayed in was called Gauting; it was picture-postcard beautiful with all the snow.

On a Monday we started work. There were two jobs on offer. A major on a C130 and minor on a Nato 707. I decide to take the 707. In hindsight, I should have taken the C130. Colby's tentacles were involved in this. All the damn time travel at the ATA snooping into the future. I had upset the Emperor and would pay the price. Colby used a snail gun. Slow but nigh on impossible to escape from. I was trapped in a Godless machine with no hope of escape. All I could do was lie to myself about it.

While I was there, I decided to use my spare time to write some new songs. I called it the Paradise Project. The plan was to write one song per week while I was working on the shop floor. My manager, Andreas, was very accommodating and a very likeable man. I enjoyed my time working with him; it was the best time I ever had on the aircraft. The day would start with a cup of coffee and a chat about the work for the day. The jobs were always small but interesting. I worked with a German engineer who was very skilled but did not speak any English. I knew a bit of German and it was enough; we worked together very well. If I came up with a song lyric, Andreas would let me stop working to write it down. I wrote one song a week; my favourite was about my old girlfriend Sally.

My accommodation this time was much better. I had a proper room in the pension and my own en suite. A far cry from the basement rooms I had had previously. I was also going out more with the others. There was a bar in the village where we used to drink. It had a mega stereo system which they were not utilising. I offered to DJ for them on a Saturday night. It went down very well. After word got round, the place was packed to the rafters. As payment, I was given 50 Marks for the night, around £17; I didn't complain, as I enjoyed doing it and people bought me drinks occasionally. After it closed, we used to go a nightclub close to the village; it stayed open until around 3:00 a.m. In all fairness, it was crap, but it was the only place to go if you wanted a drink after 11:00 p.m. Most of the clientele were male and gay. Most of them took cocaine, and none of them appeared to be enjoying themselves. The music was also dire. The most played music was cheesy 80's soft rock. It was awful but amusing. The cocaine use though was prolific. They all seemed to take it, and none of them appeared to be happy!

Chapter 11

About halfway through the contract, Lady Jane turned up. This got me worried, and I thought something serious was going on at home. I told her I would pack, but she said that was unnecessary. The others found it thrilling that such a person had come to visit. I was not so thrilled. It was a bad omen. Lady Jane left and we returned to normal, but the uneasy feeling did not go away. The song writing was going really well, and by the end of the contract, I had finished 12 songs. I was hopeful that this was my ticket to an easier and more successful life.

During the contract, there had been a problem with my bank; they were not banking my pay cheques. In hindsight, I should have gone home to sort it out, but the company rep said I would be paid in cash at the end of the contract. This was fine. A few hours before my flight, we met in a café in Munich, and he had the money for me. Then a supermodel turned up. We had a sexual encounter the year before. For reasons unknown to me, he gave her my pay; it was around £3,000 in cash. Maybe it was for the sex. My run-in with Lady Luck was starting to worry me. Things kept going wrong for me. What looked like things improving was doing the opposite. What would go wrong next?

I arrived at the airport in good time. I had a quick mooch round the airport duty free and then went to my departure gate to await my flight. It had been a long day, and I nodded off. I awoke about an hour later; I had missed my flight. Luckily, I worked for Dornier, and they got me on the next flight to Manchester, no extra charge. The reality of home was starting to sink in. I had no money to show for my exploits. Maybe the music would be my answer.

I arrived at Manchester on 1 April 1995. For a change, it was a nice day. I had about £50 in cash on me, and by luck, there was a Southport taxi outside arrivals. I asked the lady who booked it if I could share; she agreed. Something was going right, or so I thought.

I got home late afternoon to find Vince and Dean waiting for me in my flat; my stupid landlord had let them in to wait. They knew I had been writing; someone tipped them off, and I never found out who it was. They knew exactly what to take. They said they wanted two years' head start; I was in no position to argue. The music was released about four weeks later and was an instant success. It was too big for me to take on, plus I had no money and not even a phone. This hurt. I kept telling myself not to be bitter about it – the advice I gave Sally.

The flat had become more sinister now. Before, it had been monotony and attrition. Now, a new element of IT was in play: menace. A deep-rooted fear and fate closing in on me. But I did not give up. I decided to try and write myself out of it at the local library.

My usual routine, going to the Academy to work, stopped. I continued to babysit, though. I commenced work at the start of May in the local library. I went into several areas – film, music, art, audio visuals and particle physics.

I wrote several screenplays. In those days, people would bite my arm off for one of my screenplays especially after the success of *Terminator 2*. Most notable were *Men in Black*, *Independence Day*, *Phantom Menace*, *Star Trek First Contact* and *Titanic*. Titanic was my masterpiece. Or greatest delusion. It took me 10 weeks to write. The others only took me a day or two. I was confident they would pay me, but I was wrong. I did not expect any of the others to cough up, as I knew the movie business. Dog eat dog. Only the music business was worse. While doing these screenplays, I wrote a guide to screenplay writing, as I had never heard of one. I liked Anna Nicole Smith and thought she was a very caring person and very misunderstood. I gave it to her. She used it and wrote *Volcano*.

I wrote lyrics and music for the first album for the Spice Girls. The Spice Girls were the hype, with my particle theory called SPICE. I got the idea for them from a painting in a Southport art gallery. It was a picture of five young women almost bursting out of the canvas. I did quite a lot of the work for them; the image consultants did the rest. I knew they would be successful, as they had a lot of talent; but I did not expect the magnitude of their success. They were global on a massive scale. A few weeks after 'Wannabe' was released, they came to see me to say thank you. They gave me about £3,000. I knew no matter what I did, I would not be able to keep it and just gave it to my landlord as prepaid rent. I wanted to move out, but there was always something in the way; IT would not let me. Other notable songs were for Robbie Williams and Alanis Morrisette. These songs made them a success just like the Spice Girls. I never even received a thank you from them.

I was feeling particularly artistic, so I decided to do an oil painting. To prove it was my work, I did several things. I filmed myself with a video camera, and I also did an underpainting. It was a picture of myself, Frank and Anne Pasternac doing some decorating with ladders and paint pots and brushes. Then on top, I did my next masterpiece. It was a landscape-themed painting. What made it special was that it was my interpretation of the view in the eyes of a Terminator android. I chose the name 'Pousin'. It later went up for auction and made £15 million pounds. Anna Nicole Smith came to see me and told me I need to go to my bank to receive payment. I was too scared to go to the bank; I thought 'they' would kill me and that Lady Jane would take the money. This was my paranoia. And it was getting worse.

After being rich, although only momentarily, I decided that the AV equipment available was in long need of a makeover. Cathode ray tubes had been around for a good 50 years, and it was about time that they were made obsolete. So I invented the plasma TV. I sent the specs to Pioneer, and they made the first ones. I also invented digital television, 720 HD and 1080 Full HD formats using 16:9 screen ratio. VHS was long overdue for being made redundant. I came up with DVD, the digital versatile disk. In this case, I let the patents go so there would be no format war like there was with VHS and Betamax; the other patents went to the 'Company'. Four other things I came up with were the blue LED and Dolby Pro Logic II. TV was now ready for the 21st century. And also I invented the tyre pressure sensors that tell you if your tyres need inflating and MP3 digital music format.

In particle physics, I came up with a new theory, an electromagnetic map of the Standard Model. It covers time travel, teleportation and hyperdrive/wormholes. I called it SPICE, which stands for South, Pole, Interface, Collector and Energiser. This covers five properties of particles in five-dimensional space in the Standard Model. It also makes it easier to understand the relationships between the particles of the Standard Model. The theory marries up with Richard Feynman's quark theory of mesons. The scientific community took my theory as a joke, as it was only approximate, but I think they were missing the point. To know the nature of a road, you do not drill a two-mile-deep hole in it; you simply examine the surface. Using this theory, it is possible to travel faster than the speed of light. I did the maths and found the maximum speed one could travel at is 666 times the speed of light. Feynman was at least 25 years ahead of me on this. I examined it further and found I could raise this maximum speed to 700 times the speed of light. I was the first from Earth to do this calculation. This is the record; it apparently has never been beaten.

The space technology was done for Bill Clinton. It remains confidential.

I came up with a few random ideas while doing my work. The first was the Millennium Bug. From owning digital watches with the year function, I discovered that the year only went up to 1999. The millennium bug. As it turned out, there was no cause for alarm. Nothing happened, but that was the whole point!

For some reason, I took an interest in Carling Black Label advertising and designed a new advertising campaign for them. It was the diamond pump head. They paid me £25,000 in cash, but IT would not let me keep it. I gave it to a friend of my mother's daughter, Sharon, so she could finance going to university. She did thank me, which was unusual. Most people took what they wanted from me and never said thank you.

I realised that my work was too big for me, which is why I started the Company. It was to control off-world access and would be a constant while politics were changing. The main players were the UK, USA, France, Italy and Germany although the Germans went their own way and not very successfully either. On the UK side, MI5 were in charge while the CIA ran America. The Company is an Earth company, not a national concern. They are in charge of Earth's welfare in the galactic community. You are probably wondering how you get an off-world pass. It is not easy. Earth has a few starships but not many, namely, the North Star 1, Discovery 2 and 3, and that is about it. To get on the program, you need to solve the hyperdrive equation to get 700 times the speed of light. That is the first step. You cannot copy someone else's work; the Company will know.

You also need the right aptitude. The Company is always looking for new blood. To put the chances of getting off world with the Company into perspective, you have more chances of winning the National Lottery, twice! But bear in mind, all that glitters is not gold.

While I was working, a few things mysteriously appeared on my desk in the library. Most notable was what appeared to be a teleport bracelet. With my paranoia, I was too scared to use it. What would I be getting into? I was already in over my head. All I wanted was some face-to-face advice. Nobody came to talk to me. After 10 weeks of work, I decided that I had done enough. The patents would finance the Company for the foreseeable future. If you made a breakthrough and wanted in, you need to give up your patent rights to the company.

After my work was submitted to the White House and Downing Street, the offers started coming in. British Aerospace were knocking on my door. I was too ill to take any post with them. I was trapped in a mental straitjacket. I could not get out of that damn flat. I knew I had to spend five years there before 'they' would let me go. This was my sentence from Lady Jane for not pledging my allegiance to her. If you added in the time loops, I was doing 50 years at least. Andreos from Dornier also came over to see me to ask me to come back to the 707, but again, I could not take it. I could feel Colby's menacing smile as I turned down dream ticket after dream ticket. My life was a living hell.

From here on in, my life became a boring nightmare. I was on the dole and had no prospect of getting a job. IT started to have an impact on me. I did my shopping every two weeks when I got my cheque. I would go to Safeways and do my fortnightly shop. This would consist of 10 microwaved Weight Watchers meals. I could not get any more in the freezer compartment in my fridge. A block of cheese, some bread, baked beans and rice. The rest, IT made me spend it straightaway. I would go to the pub and blow it on beer and Bacardi. To someone not in the know, it would look like I was just an idiot who could not manage their money. But it was far more sinister than that. I used to tell people IT made me do it. They used to say, 'What is IT?' I could not explain. If I was lucky, my food would last me 12 days; that would mean two days of starvation. Babysitting for Kirstie and Graham helped, as they used to give me a fiver. This would also pay for tobacco. I must have weighed less than 9 stone at the time and had a 28-inch waist.

The summers were better because it was warmer in the flat. Winter was awful. I had no heating, and it was often warmer outside than in my flat. Having no TV made it soul-destroyingly boring. I would sit for hours on the bench in total silence. There was also the torture sessions. I would be beamed out and subjected to something like a cross between boiling water and electric shocks. The time loops made it worse. At first, I learned when the loops would occur and took evasive actions. But it learned from this, and the loops became random in length. It was like trench warfare. Moving forward in time was a slow laborious process with battle fatigue thrown in for good measure. I also used to hear a firing squad outside the flat. I am pretty sure that was in my head, as it stopped when I went outside.

There was one upside to all this: the women. I was regularly visited by famous supermodels, and famous women in general. They were all gorgeous. They always managed to get in my flat even when the door was locked. They must have been beamed in! We would have sex, then there would be a time loop, and they would be erased on the new timeline. There must have been about 30 of them. To be honest, I don't care if they were real or not; it was a really nice experience in all this. There were a couple of women who I believe were real: Mary and Lady Jane. The rest, I think, were just fiction.

My most prestigious visitor was Jackie Onassis. She came to see me a few weeks before her death. Her security were all over Southport, and they were all armed. I had to go to sign on that day, and she insisted that I go with a gun in a shoulder holster. I hated guns, but she made me wear it. She came to see me because she had something to tell me. It was about the assassination of JFK. It was the missing piece of the puzzle. Who sent Jack Ruby? Jackie told me she sent him to kill Lee Harvey Oswald as revenge for killing her husband. She wanted this to be released on her death. Unfortunately, by this time the psychosis was too much. People stopped listening to me. I was shunned. All they saw in me was a loser. Nobody understood what I was going through.

Lady Jane was cruel to me. She made me draw a spaceship on a piece of pink paper and told me to show it to the tellers at my bank. If you are wondering why I did this, I had no choice; her threats were scary. From then on, the bank treated me like a loony. Shortly after this, I won £500 on the lottery. I tried to bank it, but they just took it off me. There was nothing I could do about it.

The winter of 1995/1996 was bleak. I was freezing and starving, my clothes were falling off my back, my shoes had worn-out souls and 'IT' was making my life hell. I got three Christmas cards that year: Mum, Dad and Val and my Gran. It was mostly my fault that I had no friends. After finishing my work in the library, I felt I had nothing in common with my Southport friends. I called it walking around at ground zero. In the new year of 1996 madness set in. I started having conspiracy theories, which, taking a step back, were absolutely ridiculous and funny but at the time were far from funny.

The first was Operation Circus. The Moscow State Circus was visiting Southport. I believed that they were orchestrating a time-travel attack. The circus was hiding soldiers, and the tents would appear all over the country simultaneously, and they would seize power. A crazy notion, but I thought it was real.

The next one was the Excalibur programme. Scientists were experimenting with giving people three legs. I was getting three, but Lady Jane wanted six. The extra legs were a status symbol. At the time, I did not realise I was ill. Another one was that Space Hoppers made a comeback, and everyone was using them. I saw a woman in a shop using one while doing her shopping. It was total rubbish of course, but not to me.

The most interesting episode I had was a time-travel episode. Out of all of them, this one seemed the most plausible. It was mid-1996, and I stepped out of my door at Castle Close to find I was in the 1960s. It was fascinating, so I went for a walk. I went to the local shop for a nosey. If I had any sense, I would have kept on walking, but after 20 minutes, I decided to go back to my flat. I walked through my front door, and I was back in 1996 again.

The thing that finally made me realise I was really ill was seeing the Millennium Falcon flying over Southport one night in total silence on my way home from babysitting. I knew then that something was seriously wrong with me and that I needed help.

The time loops continued. One day in the summer of '96, I bought myself a bottle of Bacardi and decided to drown my sorrows for a few hours. I was about halfway through the bottle when I was beamed into that torture chamber in 1991 with Evil Dave. I was made to lie on what looked like an altar, and once I was on it, I could not move. The pain started to increase. Slowly and steadily. I felt myself going through the stages, level 1, boiling water. Level 2, boiling oil. Then level 3, hell. I think I was on there for 20 minutes. In the last few seconds, the level went up again to hell squared. I shouted, 'God save the queen!' I could feel explosions going through my body; it was over, thank God! Reece had saved me.

Next thing I remember was being back in my flat and sitting on my bed crying. Anyone who thinks being drunk under extreme pain is preferable is wrong; it made it worse. I had to get out of there. I decided to get a priest in to bless the place. It was the only thing I could think of to do about it. I went to the church on Lord Street and went to talk to the priest. He agreed to come to my flat to do the blessing. At the time, I was becoming a believer with regards to God. I figured that if the Devil existed, then it stands to reason that so does God. My faith was starting to grow. The blessing helped. The flat did not seem so terrible now.

The next few months were more bearable.

On 13 December 1996, Bill Clinton and General Schwarzkopf came to see me. This was the day of my loop. I was standing by the bar fire, dreading being sent back. I was amazed, using the Star Wars computer they replicated for me. It was the replica which was sent back. I had never been more relieved in my entire life. There was light at the end of the tunnel. They asked me who was torturing me; I was almost too scared to tell them, but Bill Clinton and General Schwarzkopf were the two men I most trusted in the whole world. I told them it was Jabba the Hutt. They got him!

The time loops continued, but now I was getting help. The younger me, the apprentice, was trying to help me. I kept playing the first track of Def Leppard's *Pyromania*, 'Rock Rock'. Every time I did this, it started another loop. Somehow I needed to warn myself in the loop so I would not do it again. I used the *Daily Express*; I used a horoscope. It read 'Fates eyes are watching you like a cat'. It worked! The looping stopped. After that all I had to do was escape the flat.

I had another crappy Christmas and then faced 1997 with a little more optimism. I needed a sign. Something to bolster my growing faith. I had a visit from Lady Jane on St Patrick's Day, and for the first time in several years, we were starting to get on with each other again. We parted on good terms. Southport theatre were showing a play called *Get Out of Here!* The poster had a picture of God on it pointing into the distance. I realised that this was it; this was my chance to escape.

Blake came calling as well. He told me he was going to torture me and then kill me, but I had the option to shoot myself in the head. I chose the second option. I could not cope with any more torture; a shot in the head would be far more preferable. I held the gun to my head and pulled the trigger. Blake jammed the hammer with his finger and took the gun off me. He looked like he got what he came for and left. I never saw him again.

On my first attempt to escape, I got about three miles down the road, then turned around. Then, on 1 May, Mayday I decided that this was my chance. I left with just the clothes I was standing in, I was going to go to London to face my destiny. I walked the first five miles, then hitched a lift with a man in a van. He dropped me off the other side of Ormskirk by the M58 at the Little Chef. I did not know what to do. I decided London was a bad idea. There was a phone box by the Little Chef, so I called the police and told them I did not know what to do and I did not want to go back to Southport. A car arrived about 10 minutes later, and they took me to Ormskirk Hospital and sat me in A&E. I waited for 20 minutes, then they took me to the psychiatric ward.

It was a notable night; it was General Election night. I had my fingers crossed that Blair would win. The MP, Mo Mowlam, came to see me, which set me off for want of a better description. I started shouting, 'Blur, beef, seven, blame the Germans!' I was now officially off my trolley. I was sectioned under section 3 of the Mental Health Act.

It was nice being in hospital. I had three meals a day, a comfortable bed, and I was warm. Castle Close was becoming a distant memory. I found a place in the hospital where I could listen to the radio and reflect away from the other patients. Robbie Williams was being played a lot, my songs 'Angels' and 'Old Before I Die'. I found these songs more uplifting than the Spice Girls songs, as every time I heard the Spice Girls, it reminded me of Castle Close.

I spent two weeks in the mental health unit at Ormskirk and then they moved me to the Park Unit in Southport. I told them I did not want to go, but I had no choice; it was my area. One of the staff from the Hesketh Centre came to pick me up. I was scared that things would start happening like time loops and famous people visiting. Luckily it did not. Lady Luck was smiling again.

I spent over four months in the Park Unit. It was situated on the first floor of the Hesketh Centre. I arrived at the Park Unit literally with nothing but the clothes I was wearing. The unit was secure, and you needed to be buzzed in and out. The unit was in two halves: accommodation and day areas.

There were about 16 patients of mixed sexes. As far as hospitals go, this was a nice place to be, and I felt lucky to be a patient there. The staff were lovely and very professional, and the food was great. Despite this, I could not wait to get discharged. As I was on a section 3, they could hold me for up to six months.

The worst part of it was my diagnosis and subsequent treatment. I was diagnosed as having paranoid schizophrenia. I was far more ill than I or my family had realised. Even my father was sympathetic when he found out. The treatment was a nightmare. In keeping with NHS policy, they tried the cheapest treatments first. They had some horrible side effects. On one of the drugs, I stayed awake for a couple of days and was aching with tiredness all the time. Another one contorted the muscles in my neck, and I had to ask for the antidote for it.

My father came to visit and asked me what I needed. I needed underwear and shoes. I was in rags. One of the doctors, Alice, took a shine to me, and she seduced me into a cupboard, and we had sex. As my treatment continued, I started to realise that this sexual encounter was probably just in my head. She knew I wrote songs and also that I knew Lady Jane. One afternoon, she asked me if there was anything I needed or wanted to do. I decide to write the second album for the Spice Girls. With the first one, I wrote lyrics and music. With the second, I only wrote the lyrics for them. I knew this would be enough; I did not want to leave them with a one-hit wonder. The songs took about an hour to write. I asked Alice to send them to Simon Fuller, but I had bigger things to worry about, so I let it go. I did it for the girls.

After about two months, I was put on Clozaril. This was the most expensive schizophrenia drug on the market at the time. It worked! This was last-chance saloon; if this did not work, I would be mentally impaired for the rest of my life. As with the others, it had side effects, but they were not too bad. It made me sleepy all the time and also gave me chronic constipation. Both were a pain in the arse; the constipation was, literally! The constipation would plague me for many years as my body eventually adjusted. It began to go away in 2012. Thankfully, the drowsiness wore off after a few years too.

The time in the Park Unit went quickly. I had a famous visitor in late May: Bill Clinton. He came to see me to see how I was doing and also to thank me personally for my work that I did for him, 'Space Technology'. He asked me if there was anything he could do for me. I knew money would be a waste of time at that time, so I asked for the commissioning of a new Star Trek series, Enterprise. I also requested a really good mirror-universe episode. A few years later they delivered. It is set on 13 January 2155, my birthday! I also unwisely asked them to fire Dave Lewis, one of my old instructors for some reason. Mr Clinton said he did not think this would be a good idea. He was right. All BA planes had their tails painted funny colours after that! After his visit, I wrote him a letter of thanks, to which he replied. This was definitely not a delusion. It helped my self-esteem and made me feel valued as a person again.

By August, I was doing very well. I had put on two and a half stone and was much better in myself. It was time to find somewhere to live. I told them point blank that I would not be returning to Castle Close. They respected this. The home finder was called in. He took me out in his BMW to look at a few flats. Anything would be better than Castle Close. I chose the flat with the best aura. Irving Street. It was privately owned, and the landlord was very nice and friendly. He was selective about who lived in his flats, so there was no riff-raff. It was partly furnished, had electric storage heating and a TV. Just the job to get me started again.

On 1 September, staff woke me with the news that Diana had died in a car crash. I was shocked and upset. I left hospital in September and started my new life. The benefits lady, Joan, had sorted out all my benefits for me. She filled in all my forms, and I was getting the equivalent income of someone on a £20,000 salary. I never went out, so I saved quite a bit of money. Although I had been released, I was still a long way from being well again. This would take years.

I was put in the care of the outreach team and met other people with mental health issues and schizophrenia. I made a few friends, and it kept me busy and feeling included. The thing I enjoyed the most was therapeutic woodwork. The NHS had a workshop in Ainsdale, and I went there twice a week. We made garden furniture and odds and sods to order. I enjoyed it, as it reminded me of my metal-working skills; I also took pride in my work. There were other activities there too: they had a full-size snooker table, and we used to play Boule on a patch of gravel. The place was supervised by

Mike and Andy; they were very nice people and very understanding, and they helped me a lot with my recovery.

Chapter 12

I found myself with a lot of time on my hands. My recovery was long and slow. Although I had been released from hospital, it did not mean I was well again by any stretch of the imagination. I suffered from acute anxiety especially in social situations, and I had stopped drinking alcohol all together. Watching television was my only escape. My musical tastes had also changed; I started to like pop songs, and my interest in rock had diminished probably because it reminded me of when I was really ill. I was also very easily pleased, which was a good thing. Since being diagnosed, I took a vow of celibacy, something I later regretted. I had no social circle outside of my family and the CMHT (Community Mental Health Team), but I was happy, I felt safe and nothing weird or out of the ordinary was happening for the first time in as long as I can remember. IT was a distant memory.

After a year of recovery, I made my first step back into normal life. With not going out, I saved quite a bit of money from my benefits. I started to learn to drive. I decided to go with a local instructor rather than a large franchise. It was called Halifax. I picked it because I liked the name, no other reason. I had two lessons a week before I was ready for the test. I did 15 lessons in all. I passed my test first time.

My father and step mum Val took me car shopping. I could afford no more than £1,750. We looked at a few my father considered to be death traps, and we decided to get a red Mini City 1000cc. I hindsight, it was a piece of crap. It had just reached the tipping point of rampant corrosion. It had about 30,000 miles on the clock, but after I bought it, I got the feeling that it had either been clocked or had gone round the clock. It needed servicing every six months, as bits kept falling off it. I regretted buying it; it was not the Mini we expected. I kept it for five years, as I could not afford to buy anything else. It was a money pit.

I decided that I had enough of doing nothing. In the summer of 1999, the CMHT found me a voluntary work placement at a training centre on Shakespeare Street. I went a couple of times a week. The job mostly involved photocopying. What was interesting was what they were doing. They were teaching unemployed people computer skills. I decided that this is what I wanted to do, so I went back to college and did some computer courses. Why not? It was free, as I was on benefits. I was also referred to a charitable trust. They specialised in working with disadvantaged adults to gain employment. Great!

The trust office was based in Bootle, Liverpool. The first time I went down there, I got the train. It took about 35 minutes. There I met my development officer, Win. She was a lovely lady and reminded me of the dark-haired singer in ABBA. I told her I wanted to get back into work, but I made it clear that I did not under any circumstances want to go back to the aerospace industry. I told her I was interested in computers, and that is what I wanted to do.

The first thing was to get on new courses ASAP. I had done CLAIT at Southport College and was working on Integrated Business Technology levels 2 and 3. The first thing she did was to get me on an NVQ 2 in software creation. This was two days a week and in Litherland. I drove there in my Mini twice a week. This was the first time since the early '90s that I needed my social skills. There were three of us on the course: Mick and John and myself. The object of the exercise was to create a jukebox programme using Visual Basic and SQL code. This my first introduction into modern object-based programming. It was called Basic, but there was nothing basic about it. I learned a lot, but after three months, I was wishing I'd done the maintenance course instead. Mick and John said the same thing. The skills would have been far more useful.

I completed the course in six months, and Win was pleased. I had shown her that I could stick at something. Win offered me a voluntary position at the trust in the IT training department 16 hours per week. I took it. They paid my train fare and lunch. The manager, Teresa, became a good friend. I worked four days, helping Doug, my mentor, to deliver CLAIT. I took to it like a duck to water, and I found I enjoyed it; it was very rewarding work. At that time, with the trust, we mostly supported learning difficulties and mental health clients. Things went really well. I finally had some purpose in my life again.

From 1999 to January 2002, nothing happened except my placement. There was no sex with stars, no clandestine visits by prime ministers and presidents, no spaceships and no time travel or teleportation. I had found my Ordinary World. Home was good too. I liked my flat even though it was tiny and on a dingy street; my neighbours were all respectable and friendly as was the landlord, Alan. These were happy, if uneventful, times. The time went quickly, but big change was on the horizon.

In January 2002, it was time for my mental health review with the DSS doctor at Merton House. I knew my number was up because I had been doing so well, so it was no surprise that they marked me down as eligible to work and put me on job seekers allowance. This was a heavy blow. I started job hunting in earnest. I had a few interviews for fairly basic jobs using my computer skills but had no joy. I continued at the Trust doing my voluntary work, but the job centre seemed to frown on it. After 10 months, the pressure of the job centre was getting to me. I had to fill in a book every day to demonstrate my job seeking. I was hoping the trust would take me on, but this was looking like a pipe dream. In late November, I got a job offer from Marks and Spencer to do shelf stacking. I was about to resign myself and then got some good news. The trust would like to take me on as a training and placement officer, but it was part time.

I was invited to a meeting with Teresa. She told me that they were prepared to offer me a part-time post as a training and placement officer. I told her it would need to be full time for financial reasons because of travel expenses. Teresa agreed. I was offered the start date of 6 December 2002.

Shortly after I started, we moved offices to Hawthorne Road, Bootle. So it was all change for the rest of the staff as well. I was relieved and happy that I had landed this job and felt very lucky, as I had been only one step away from shelf stacking!

The new premises were a large Victorian house that had previously been used as a gym. It needed all the wiring redoing and network connections installing. We had two IT rooms that could hold eight and five students, but our equipment was old. There was also a training room in the basement for PDT (personal development training). My job was as a teacher for adult learners. I finished my City and Guilds 7307 Teaching Adult Learners in September.

On my first day, I was sent to the Liverpool office to deliver an English class for young adults. I could not have asked for a better bunch of students. The lesson went very well. Teresa was pleased.

At Hawthorne Road, I worked with my mentor Doug. He was about 15 years my senior. We delivered CLAIT and Business Technology level 2. CLAIT was easy, Business Technology was not. You had to be really on the ball to teach this one. To make the job harder, everyone worked at their own pace, so everyone was on a different page. It kept me very busy; it was also quite stressful, but I took it in stride.

PDT (personal development training) was fun. This was a course for young adults with learning difficulties. It was a six-month course using units I devised myself. Travel training was prominent as was skills around money. They were mostly a pleasure to teach, but we did get bad apples from time to time who would bully the other students, especially when there were no staff about. When we got rid of one, another one would arrive. This kept me on my toes.

Over time, the job evolved and got harder and harder. My other job was delivering EAI (enhanced advice intervention). This was a pain in the neck. It was worth £5,000 a year, and it was a pig. The people from EAI were good cop, bad cop. The way we were scrutinised was what you would expect from a £500,000 contract, not £5,000! My work was always poor in their eyes. It was very frustrating. Annually we would be re-interviewed for our jobs; this was across the board. My manager, Lindsay, asked me an EAI question, and I gave her the best answer she had ever heard. I felt vindicated after the poor reviews from EAI.

I did this job for eight and a half years. In Christmas 2010, I was informed that I would be made redundant. I took the news with trepidation, but I need not have worried; I found a new job straightaway. The money was not as good, but it was in Southport, so no commuting. I was given a reasonable redundancy package.

My last day was Friday, 13 May 2011. I finished around 3:00 p.m. and shared the journey home with my colleague, Brian. On the way into Southport on the Coast Road, we decided to stop to look at something we had been driving past together for the last two years. It was a model of an aeroplane in the middle of a roundabout. There was a display panel facing the aeroplane, so we stopped to see what it was about. Would you believe it was about transatlantic flights from Southport to New York? They started service on Friday, 13 May 1932! What an amazing coincidence. It made me wonder if some time travel had been involved in this. It was quite a fluke. It may be a trip I haven't made yet that determined this, but I took it as a good omen.

Not only was I changing jobs, but I was also changing residence. I was moving out of Irving Street after 14 years. I had a new flat just yards away from Irving Street with a much nicer aspect. This flat was a vast improvement from the old one. Also, there was no damp; there was fungal damp at Irving Street, which gave me breathing problems. It had double glazing, gas central heating, nice kitchen and bathroom and a single-bed room. I was out of bedsit land. I moved in the weekend after finishing at the trust, and some of my friends came down to help. I felt truly at home for the first time in years. Gas central heating was just a dream on Irving Street. I used to spend a fortune on electricity; keeping one room warm, I could now stay cosy and warm all winter at a fraction of the cost. I was very happy.

Since then, I have had one episode. September 2012. I was picked up by North Star One and did the trip to Blackpool 1960s mentioned earlier. There have been no episodes since. Maybe it was the medication, maybe it was the end of an era or maybe it was a mixture of both. I don't know. I never saw Mary, Lady Jane or Reece again.

Available worldwide from

Amazon

---

www.mtp.agency

www.facebook.com/mtp.agency

@mtp_agency

Printed in Great
Britain
by Amazon

31495697R00125